D1554234

San Jose Bible College
Memorial Library

Presented by

Friends
In Memory Of

CLE KENNEDY

1911-1970

STUDIES IN PROBLEM TEXTS

THE BOOKS OF J. SIDLOW BAXTER

AWAKE, MY HEART
Daily devotional meditations for the entire year. These readings are "beautifully simple and simply beautiful, profoundly simple and simply profound." — *Evangelical Christian*

GOING DEEPER
A deeply spiritual study on the theme of knowing, loving and serving our Lord Jesus Christ.

HIS PART AND OURS
Enriching exposition and devotional studies in the reciprocal union of Christ and His people. "A truly great book."
— *Moody Monthly*

GOD SO LOVED
A captivating new presentation of John 3:16. Theological, devotional, practical. In two parts —. (1) The New Testament Truth, (2) The Old Testament Type.

STUDIES IN PROBLEM TEXTS
Informing, elucidatory and applicatory expositions of certain Scripture passages which have occasioned perplexity.

MARK THESE MEN
Arresting studies in striking aspects of Bible characters with special relevances for our own times and the days ahead.

EXPLORE THE BOOK
A notable work on the Bible; in one handsome volume of approximately 1800 pages, 6 volumes in one.

THE STRATEGIC GRASP OF THE BIBLE
A series of studies in the structural and dispensational characteristics of the Bible.

STUDIES
IN PROBLEM TEXTS

*Being a short series of elucidatory and
applicatory expositions of certain Scripture
passages which have occasioned perplexity*

J. SIDLOW BAXTER

ZONDERVAN PUBLISHING HOUSE
GRAND RAPIDS, MICHIGAN

First printing......1960
Second printing....1963
Third printing 1968
Fourth printing....1970

Printed in the United States of America

FOREWORD

How MUCH we owe, many of us, to the problem texts of the Bible! What hours of profitable searching and study they have provoked! How they have disciplined us in patience and painstaking investigation!

And how endlessly interesting these problem texts make the Bible! Joseph Parker well said: "When the last word has been said about the Bible it will no longer be the Word of God." We never get to the end of the Bible. It is as wise in its reservations as in its revelations. Enough is revealed to make faith intelligent. Enough is reserved to give faith scope for development. Everything needful to salvation and godliness is written with such clarity that all the simple-hearted may understand; but there are other matters which, with wise divine purpose, are presented less lucidly, or even enigmatically, so as to challenge enquiry— matters fascinating, mysterious, or more intricate, but all yielding rich and sanctifying reward to devout exploration.

The following chapters pick merely on a dozen or so of these problem texts, and even these few are treated only briefly, except in the case of the final chapter. It may be wondered why the final study is so much longer than the others. There are three reasons. First, it really deals with four problem texts all in one. Second, it is a subject as complicated as it is intriguing. Third, we did not wish to discourage the reader by putting this much lengthier article in the earlier part of the book.

We have not forgotten to make practical applications of the matters herein discussed, for the theoretical divorced from the practical is valueless. If these studies stir up in any reader a keener interest in the study of the inspired Word, our writing will be well rewarded.

J. S. B.

DEDICATION

IT IS with sincerest appreciation and esteem
that I dedicate these "Studies in Problem
Texts" to the Elders of Charlotte Baptist
Chapel, Edinburgh, a "band of men whose
hearts God has touched", whose genial good-
will, wise counsel and co-operative com-
panionship in the pre-war, mid-war and
post-war years has meant more than words
can say.

J. S. B.

CONTENTS

"RIVERS OF LIVING WATER"

—John vii. 37–9.

"RIVERS OF LIVING WATER"

"In the last day, that great day of the feast, Jesus stood and cried, saying, If any man thirst, let him come unto Me, and drink. He that believeth on Me, as the Scripture hath said, out of his belly shall flow rivers of living water. (But this spake He of the Spirit which they that believe on him should receive: for the Holy Spirit was not yet given, because that Jesus was not yet glorified.)" John vii. 37-9.

THIS arresting utterance, which rang out in sonorous tones from the uplifted voice of Jesus, has been a favourite text with speakers at conventions for the deepening of the spiritual life; and convention audiences have uniformly been taught that the "rivers of living water" here spoken of are the gracious influences which emanate from the heart and life of the Spirit-filled believer. If that is what our Lord's words really teach here, however, there is one little clause which must have occasioned misgiving in most preachers' minds, and in the minds of thoughtful hearers as well. In fact, several have expressed their perplexity about it in our own hearing; and on looking up the usual Commentaries, we find that they also betray dubiety on the point. We refer to that little clause, *"as the Scripture hath said."*

"He that believeth on Me, *as the Scripture hath said*, out of him shall flow rivers of living water." But *where* does the Scripture say that "rivers of living water" should flow forth from the Christian believer? When our Lord inserted this clause, "as the Scripture hath said," He was referring to what *we* now call the Old Testament Scriptures. Where, then, in the Old Testament do we find such a prediction?

The Commentators are hard put to for an answer. The late Dr. H. W. Watkins, of Durban, in Ellicott's Commentary, says: "The exact words, 'Out of his belly shall flow rivers of living water' are not found in any part of the canonical Scriptures of the Old Testament, and yet Christ utters them with the formula of quotation. This will be a difficulty only to those who value

letter and syllable above spirit and substance. It may be that
the words which our Lord actually uttered in the current language of Jerusalem were nearer to the very words of some passage
than they seem to be in the Greek form in which St. John has
preserved them to us." We have a high regard for Bishop Ellicott
as a commentator, and therefore can express our chagrin the
more feelingly that such doubtful comments should have come
via his pages. To say that the words, "as the Scripture hath
said," are a difficulty "only to those who *value letter and syllable
above spirit and substance*," and then to suggest that "*the Greek
form*" in which John has preserved our Lord's utterance may
be loosely inexact, looks dangerously like disrespect both to our
Lord and to the Apostle John, besides being a double blow against
the orthodox view as to the inspiration of Holy Scripture.

Dr. H. W. Watkins' problem here is felt by commentators *in
general*, though their *comments* may not be so severe as his. Some
have proposed to connect the words, "as the Scripture hath said,"
with what precedes instead of with what follows, so that the
sense becomes, "He that believeth on Me, as the Scripture hath
said he must believe. . . ." But there are fatal objections to
this. Our Lord's quotation formula "as the Scripture hath
said," has to do with the "living *water*" as the counterpart of
His invitation to "*drink*"; and the best Greek scholars are
definite that the construction obliges us to take the words with
what *follows*, namely, "out of him shall flow rivers of living
water."

What then can the commentators say? The following quotation may be taken as representative: "Jesus probably intended
to say, not that there was any particular place in the Old Testament that affirmed this in so many words, but that this was the
substance of what the Scriptures taught, or this was the *spirit* of
their declarations." Well, we certainly do not like an "explanation" which has to lean back on what Jesus "*probably intended
to say*," seeing that John tells us what He actually *did* say; but
there is a far bigger objection than this, namely, that the flowing
of "living waters" from Christian believers is not even the
"*substance*" or "*spirit*" of the Old Testament Scriptures. No
such doctrine is found *anywhere* in the Old Testament. Nor,
indeed, *could* it very well be, when we reflect on it, for the Church

of the New Testament is nowhere the subject of Old Testament prophecy. The Church is a "mystery" which was "*hid*" from Old Testament generations, and only revealed through Paul and the New Testament prophets (Eph. iii. 3–10; Col. i. 24–6). It may be *latently* present in Old Testament type and foreshadowing, but it is nowhere the subject of direct statement. No, the Old Testament does not teach anywhere that these "rivers of living water" should flow from Christian believers of the present dispensation.

Look, then, once again at the words: "He that believeth on Me, as the Scripture hath said, out of him shall flow rivers of living water." Is there a real solution of the problem? *There is*, and it is really a very simple one. It has to do with the *punctuation* of the text. Our English punctuation of the Scriptures is not a part of original inspiration. If, then, we make a simple alteration in the punctuation of John vii. 37, 38, we get a transforming result which undoubtedly gives the correct presentation of our Lord's words, and at once clears away our problem.

Take the first part of our Lord's utterance: "If any man thirst, let him come unto Me, and drink." Instead of the comma after the "Me," put a full stop, or at least a semi-colon, and simply read—

> "*If any man thirst, let him come unto Me.*"

In the words which follow, the expression, "he that believeth," is a participle in the Greek—"the one believing"; so we will read on accordingly—

> "*And the one believing on Me, let him drink.*"

Note the emphasis on the "*ME*" (Christ). Now read on again —"As the Scripture hath said, out of *HIM* (Christ) shall flow rivers of living water." Now take the full utterance—

> "*If any man thirst, let him come unto ME; and let him drink who believeth on ME! As the Scripture hath said, out of HIM (the Christ) shall flow rivers of living water.*"

That, we submit, is the true way to read our Lord's words here. Surely, if it were not that we have grown so accustomed to the way the words are given in our Authorised and Revised Versions, we should realise at once how odd it is that this glorious fulness of living water should be said to flow from ourselves, and not from Christ Himself! As soon as we read the words in the re-punctuated way, we notice that their setting *confirms* our amended reading. The invitation is to those who "thirst," and, as anybody can see, our Saviour's inducement to all such would be that *their own* thirst should be quenched, not that they should *give out* rivers of water to satisfy *others*! Moreover, John's comment on our Saviour's words is: "This spake He of the Spirit which they that believe on Him should *receive*"—mark, "should *RECEIVE*," not give out to others. Clearly, and most naturally, the one thought all through our Lord's utterance and John's comment upon it is that the thirsting one who "drinks" (i.e., "believes") on *CHRIST* "receives" the living waters which flow from *CHRIST HIMSELF*. And certainly, if this was *not* the simple meaning of our Lord's utterance, then it would be practically unintelligible to those Jerusalem crowds to whom it was meant to be a clear call.

It is reassuring to have the authority of a front-rank New Testament scholar for our emended punctuation. Stier, in his *Words of the Lord Jesus*, ably advocates it. Alford does not accept Stier's alteration, but his stickling is simply the demand for a certain nicety of construction. As a matter of fact, the reshaping of the clauses brings out the evidently intended parallel between the two parts of our Lord's invitation, thus—

"If any man *THIRST*, let him *COME* unto Me";
"And let him *DRINK*, who *BELIEVETH* in Me."

There is parallelism here. The word "thirst" in the first line parallels with "drink" in the second; and "come" in the first parallels with "believeth" in the second.

Alford himself has to admit that the other punctuation is beset with difficulties; and Stier weightily rebuts Alford's note, in a later edition of his own great work on the words of the Lord Jesus. So, then, we now read the text:

"If any man thirst, let him come unto Me; and let him drink who believeth in Me. As the Scripture hath said, out of HIM (Christ) shall flow rivers of living water."

But, most important and conclusive of all, as soon as we read our text with the emended punctuation, and understand that the "living waters" flow from CHRIST, not from the one who believes, the troublesome words, "as the Scripture hath said," remain troublesome no longer; for the Old Testament again and again expresses the idea of these "living waters" in connection with the coming Christ. Take a few of the more obvious instances:

"A Man (the coming Messiah) shall be . . . as rivers of water in a dry place."—Isaiah xxxii. 2.
"Ho, every one that thirsteth, come ye to the waters. . . . Behold I have given him (the coming Messiah) for a witness to the people."—Isaiah lv. 1, 4.
"They shall look upon me whom they have pierced, and . . . in that day there shall be a fountain opened to the house of David."—Zechariah xii. 10, xiii. 1.
"And his feet shall stand in that day upon the mount of Olives. . . . And it shall be in that day, that living waters shall go out from Jerusalem."—Zechariah xiv. 4, 8.

These are a few references from the prophets; but there is also that outstanding incident in Exodus, in which rivers of water gush from the smitten rock, to slake the people's thirst. "Thou shalt smite the rock, and there shall come water out of it, that the people may drink" (Exod. xvii. 6). In 1 Corinthians x. 4 the Holy Spirit explicitly says, through Paul, "That rock was Christ," thus confirming, and at the same time amplifying, what the Jews had always somehow sensed, namely, that the rock from which the water then flowed was symbolic of Jehovah Himself, as the rock of Israel and the sustainer of His people. What that rock was really preaching to them was that "out of HIM (CHRIST) shall flow rivers of living water."

Surely these considerations seem to make it conclusive that our emended punctuating of John vii. 37, 38, is right. It is from CHRIST, not the believer (except in a very secondary way), that

these "rivers of living water" flow. And what a glorious Christ
it makes Him! Here is an ever-fresh and ever-flowing fulness
to satisfy all the spiritual thirst of human souls! It is no mere
trickling stream; but "rivers." It is no mere static pool of dead
water, but "living" waters, fresh, sweet, pure, life-bringing!
What a lovely picture to the thirsty and drought-plagued! What
a wonderful Saviour and Satisfier!

THE HISTORICAL SETTING

But now let us see and hear these arresting words of Jesus in
their circumstantial setting. As the first verse of John vii tells
us, Jesus had gone up to the "Feast of Tabernacles" at Jerusalem.
Expositors seem to be unanimous that it was part of the ritual
of this "feast" which prompted our Lord to use the metaphor
of "living waters."

There were three great, annual, national "feasts" in the Jewish
religious calendar. These were (1) the Feast of the Passover,
which fell in the first month of the year, corresponding roughly
to our own April, and lasted eight days; (2) the Feast of Pentecost,
which began fifty days after the end of the Passover, hence its
name, *Pentekostos*, the Greek ordinal for fiftieth; (3) the Feast
of Tabernacles, which ran from the fifteenth to the twenty-second
day of the seventh month, that is, some four months after Pentecost, and therefore at the end of the harvest season. The original
institution of these "Feasts of Jehovah" is found in Leviticus
xxiii, with emphasising references, also, in Exodus xxiii. 14–16,
and Deuteronomy xvi. 16.

The Feast of Tabernacles, or Booths, was so-called because
during it the people were to live in booths of branches and leaves.
This is what we read in the original institution, in Leviticus xxiii.
40–3:

"And ye shall take you, on the first day, the boughs of goodly
trees, branches of palm trees, and the boughs of thick trees,
and willows of the brook; and ye shall rejoice before Jehovah
your God seven days. . . . Ye shall dwell in booths seven
days; all that are Israelites born shall dwell in booths; that
your generations may know that I made the children of

Israel to dwell in booths when I brought them out of the land of Egypt."

So this dwelling in booths spoke of freedom after bondage, of God's intervention for deliverance, of His wonderful provision for them in their wilderness journeyings, and of their temporary pilgrim-dwellings during that time. This "feast" was still observed in our Lord's time; and, as it came round year by year, all distinctions of rank and wealth were for the time being forgotten, while rich and poor alike dwelt in their little huts of leafy branches.

But this Feast of Tabernacles was also the feast of the harvest ingathering. Its alternative name, "the Feast of Ingathering," is found in Exodus xxiii. 16. This gave it an additional colourfulness and joyfulness. Dr. Marcus Dodds has well described it as follows:

"This feast was a kind of national harvest home. It was a feast, therefore, full of rejoicing. Every Israelite appeared in holiday attire, bearing in his hands a palm branch, or wearing some significant emblem of earth's fruitfulness. At night the city was brilliantly illuminated, especially round the Temple, in which great lamps, used only on these occasions, were lit, and which possibly occasioned our Lord's remark at this time, as reported in the following chapter, 'I am the light of the world.' There can be little doubt that when, on the last day of the feast, He stood and cried, 'If any man thirst, let him come unto Me,' the form of His invitation was moulded by one of the customs of the feast. For one of the most striking features of the feast was the drawing of water, in a golden vessel, from the Pool of Siloam, and carrying it in procession to the Temple, where it was poured out with such a burst of triumph from the trumpets of the Levites, aided by the Hallelujahs of the people, that it became a common Jewish saying, 'He who has not seen the rejoicing at the pouring out of the water from the pool of Siloam has never seen rejoicing in his life.' This pouring out of the water before God seemed to be an acknowledgment of His goodness in watering the corn-lands and pastures, and also a commemoration of the miraculous supply of water in the desert; while to some of the more enlightened it bore also a spiritual significance, and recalled the words of Isaiah, 'With joy shall ye draw water out of the wells of salvation.' "

Each day of the feast, at the time of the morning sacrifice, this symbolic ceremonial took place. The appointed priests brought into the Temple forecourt the golden vessel containing the water from the spring of Siloam, which rises within the mount on which the Temple stood, and poured it, along with sacrificial wine, into two bowls which stood upon the altar, and in each of which there was an opening by which the liquid made its way down to the base of the altar. Into the bowl on the eastern side of the altar the wine was poured, and simultaneously the water was poured into that on the western side, the people meanwhile shouting to the officiating priest to raise his hand, so as to show clearly that he poured the water into the bowl.

Try to recapture that historic scene, that electric moment, when the vibrant voice of Jesus rang out with startling sudden-ness over the assembled multitude. We are told that it was on "the last day, that great day of the feast." There is some diver-gence of opinion as to which day is here meant by the "last" day, because although the dwelling in booths was quite definitely for seven days only, the next day after these seven was also a "solemn assembly" in which no "servile work" was to be done (Lev. xxiii. 36; Num. xxix. 35). The point is of some interest because on the eighth day the ceremony of the water-pouring, which presumably evoked our Lord's metaphor of the "living waters," was omitted, as were other of the special rejoicings. However, Dr. Edersheim, in his great work, *Jesus the Messiah*, seems to have brought arguments which settle the matter in favour of the *seventh* day, which day, besides marking strictly the end of the "feast" and the dwelling in booths, certainly was the *great* day of the feast, a climax-point marked by special observances such as that the procession of chanting priests cir-cuited the altar seven times instead of just once as on the other days. This seventh and last day was known as that of "the Great Hosannah." As the people left the Temple, they shook off the leaves of their willow-branches around the altar, amid acclamations of thanksgiving, and beat their palm-branches to pieces. Later the same day they dismantled their booths, and thus the seven days of the "feast" ended.

Get the scene, then, on this last and "great" day of the feast.
There is the crowded assembly. Many among them are true
worshippers who have seen a spiritual meaning in that daily
ceremony of the water-pouring, and are only too conscious of
an unquenched thirst in their own hearts. There are thirsting
souls and thinking minds in that vast crowd, who have wondered each day, during the water-pouring rite, when the fountain
of waters foretold by the prophets should burst forth from the
Temple itself. But the last day of yet another annual feast has
come, and the inward longings and wistful wonderings remain
unanswered. The final forthpouring of the water has just taken
place; there has broken forth the singing of the great *Hallel*
(Psalms cxiii–cxviii) in responsive chorus, with the people waving
their palm and myrtle and citron branches toward the altar as
they sing, "Oh, give thanks unto the Lord"; and now there is
the short pause to prepare the festive sacrifices—a short pause
of stillness and silence. Just at this sensitive, strategic point,
at this one and only moment when it *could* happen with any
propriety, the unexpected happens. Suddenly, startlingly, electri-
fyingly, amid that sensitive silence, there rings out, in rich, round
tones, vibrant, sonorous, and penetrating throughout the Temple,
the voice of Jesus!—"*If any man thirst, let him come unto Me! And
let him drink who believeth on Me! For as the Scripture hath said,
out of HIM (the coming Messiah) shall flow rivers of living water.*"

It requires no vivid imagination to realize the terrific effect of
those quivering syllables; yet there was no rudeness of improper
intrusion on the part of Jesus, for, as Dr. Edersheim remarks,
"He interrupted not the services; they had for the moment
ceased: He interpreted, and He fulfilled them."

Everybody in that vast crowd would appreciate in a flash the
strategic opportunism of those arresting words at that special
moment. Many, too, would note the contrast between the "rivers
of living water" promised by Jesus and the mere vessel-full of
water brought from the Pool of Siloam to the Temple altar. But
the thing which would most of all impress them, as it has impressed men since, would be the august and tremendous implication
of the words in relation to Jesus Himself. Who, but Jesus, could
make such a claim, without absurdity or blasphemy? "If any
man thirst, let him come unto Me"—this is a claim to be the

satisfier of the universal human heart! It is stupendous; and yet somehow it falls with utter propriety from those wonderful lips. Not one Jew in that Temple concourse would fail to appreciate that in these words Jesus of Nazareth was assuming himself to be the promised Messiah; yet there is even more than that involved in the words: Jesus here speaks out of the consciousness of a divine fulness which can only belong to one who is himself, in the unique and eternal sense, *the very Son of God*.

And Jesus still stands, as He did that day, and says to the children of men—

"If any man thirst, let him come unto ME; and let him drink who believeth on ME! As the Scripture hath said, out of HIM shall flow rivers of living water."

It is interesting just to note that when our Lord says, "Let him come" and "Let him drink" he uses the present, continuous tense of the verb. We are to keep on coming, and keep on drinking. There are "rivers"; there is never any failing of the flow; we cannot come too often; we can never be disappointed! "Ho, every one that thirsteth, come ye to the waters!"

And what *is* this "living water" which Jesus offers? We are left in no doubt whatever. There is an explanatory Apostolic note subjoined to our Lord's utterance: "*This spake He of the Spirit, which they that believe on Him should receive; for the Holy Spirit was not yet given, because that Jesus was not yet glorified*" (verse 39). So these "rivers of living water" are the Holy Spirit, poured forth at Pentecost. The first promise which Pentecostal Christianity ever made to men was just this: "Repent, and be baptized every one of you in the name of Jesus Christ for the remission of sins, *AND YE SHALL RECEIVE THE GIFT OF THE HOLY SPIRIT*" (Acts ii. 38). This is the Christian secret of a life and love, of a joy and peace, of a spiritual fulness and satisfaction, which the world can neither give nor take away. This is the "life more abundant," the "joy unspeakable and full of glory," the "peace which passeth all understanding," which Jesus came to give us. Oh, that we all may drink of these life-giving, heavenly streams, drink again and again, drink deeply and really satisfyingly! "Hallelujah, what a Saviour!"

Oh, the more one looks at these words of Jesus the more wonderful they become! Millions have proved their spiritual reality. He is the everlasting fountain and fulness which answers all our need for evermore. Listen to that heavenly voice once again—"If any man thirst, let him come unto ME! As the Scripture hath said, out of HIM shall flow rivers of living water."

> I heard the voice of Jesus say,
> "Behold I freely give
> The living water, thirsty one,
> Stoop down, and drink, and live."
> I came to Jesus, and I drank
> Of that life-giving stream;
> My thirst was quenched, my soul revived,
> And now I live in Him.

"THAT ROCK WHICH FOLLOWED"

—1 Corinthians x. 4.

"THAT ROCK WHICH FOLLOWED"

"They drank of that spiritual Rock that followed them: and that Rock was Christ." 1 Corinthians x. 4.

THIS verse has been a problem not only to the ordinary reader of Scripture, but to commentators and expositors as well. Like the context in which it occurs, it looks back to the Old Testament account of the Israelite exodus from Egypt. Let us just glance backward and forward, and see the verse in its context again. Here are the first six verses of the chapter—

"Moreover, brethren, I would not that ye should be ignorant, how that all our fathers were under the cloud; and all passed through the sea; and did all eat the same spiritual meat; and did all drink the same spiritual drink; for they drank of that spiritual Rock that followed them: and that Rock was Christ. But with many of them God was not well pleased, for they were overthrown in the wilderness. Now these things were our examples [or, types to ourselves], to the intent that we should not lust after evil things as they also lusted."

We only need to turn back to Exodus xvii to read what happened in connection with "that Rock." The people were beset with thirst, and were murmuring rebelliously. God instructed Moses to take his rod, and to strike the rock in Horeb; and from that smitten rock water gushed forth to supply the people's need. But the problem about Paul's comment upon this, in 1 Corinthians x. 4, is that the rock is said by him to have "followed them"—"They drank of that spiritual Rock that *followed them.*" What shall we say about *that*? The picture of that rock *following* them is certainly difficult for one's imagination.

WHAT DO THE COMMENTATORS SAY?

What have the commentators to say about it? Well, perhaps we had better begin with *Jewish* comment—with that earliest collection of comments on the Old Testament Scriptures, namely, the *Midrash*. (The *"Midrashim"* were commentings on Scripture —mainly oral for some time—which date back to the days of Ezra and the return of the Jewish Remnant from the Babylonian exile. These "Midrashim" or explanatory amplifications gradually developed into two sorts—(1) the *Halachoth,* which sought to propound the Pentateuch as to *civil and legal* matters; and (2) the *Hagadoth,* which expanded the Scriptures homiletically and with a view to stimulating morality and virtue.) Now the Jewish *Hagadah* on Exodus xvii says that the rock itself actually followed the Israelites in their wanderings. The rabbis said that the rock was round, and rolled itself up like a swarm of bees, and that when the tabernacle was pitched, the rock came and settled in the vestibule, and began to send forth water again when the princes of Israel came before it and sang the words which we find later in Numbers xxi. 17—"Spring up, O well; sing ye unto it."

The "Pulpit Commentary," than which, in my own judgment, there is no better general commentary, disappointingly avers that in 1 Corinthians x. 4 there can be "little or no doubt" that Paul refers to this "common Jewish Hagadah." Another trusty expositor, C. J. Ellicott, after referring to "a Jewish tradition that the Rock—i.e., a fragment broken off from the rock smitten by Moses—followed the Israelites through their journey," makes what seems to me the rather strange and dangerous comment that "Paul, for the purpose of illustration, adopts that account instead of the statement in Numbers xx. 11"!

Dear old Adam Clarke characteristically explores *all* the apparent solutions—(1) that Paul speaks of the rock metonymically, that is, by the rock he means the *water* which flowed from it, and that it was the *water,* not the rock itself, which followed the people in their journeyings; (2) that by the idea of the rock *following* them we are simply meant to understand their having carried supplies of its waters with them in the usual vessels; (3) that the actual rock did itself move with them from one to another of their thirty-eight halting-places. Dr. Clarke chooses for himself the second of these "explanations"; but to ourselves it seems feeble in the extreme. Just fancy saying that the rock *"followed them"* simply because they filled their skin-bottles before leaving it there, in Horeb! No, Dr. Clarke, that will not do!

That learned and skilful commentator, Bishop Wordsworth, hits on another idea. Here are his own words: "As the psalmist and Isaiah testify, the Israelites had water flowing from the rocks in the wilderness as an *habitual consequence* of the once smiting of the rock at Horeb (see Ps. lxxviii. 15, 20, cv. 41, cxiv. 8; Neh. ix. 15; Isa. xliii. 20, xlviii. 21)." The bracketed references, however, in our own judgment, give no support at all to the bishop's "explanation." Look them up and see!

Saddest of all is the comment of the late Dean Alford, that giant among our Greek scholars and New Testament exegetes. He says, on 1 Corinthians x. 4: "It is hardly possible here, without doing violence to the words and construction, to deny that the Apostle has adopted the tradition current among the Jews, that the rock followed the Israelites in their journeyings, and gave forth water all the way." Then, realizing the seriousness of this compromise, he adds, with pathetic bravery, "And I cannot consent to depart from what appears to me the only admissible sense of these words." So, according to Alford, the divinely inspired Paul here lapses into the credulity of adopting a fantastic Jewish tradition! That, to us, is a blot on Alford's great commentary.

We need not give further examples from the commentators. They would only induce us the more to exclaim, "All they like sheep have gone astray!" One thing is very clear—they are all puzzled by the words, "That spiritual Rock that *followed them.*" Is there, then, any *further* light on this problem-text? Yes, we think there is.

WHAT DOES SCRIPTURE REALLY SAY?

First, we may settle it in our minds, once for all, that the actual rock itself did not follow the Israelites. There is nothing in the Old Testament account to give the slightest basis for such a supposition; and the grotesque invention of the Jewish *Midrash* must be categorically denied.

Second, despite all the commentators, *Paul does not say that the rock followed the Israelites!* That may sound rather startling.

Surely the words are there, clearly enough, in 1 Corinthians x. 4
—"That spiritual Rock that *followed them*"! Yes, the words are
there, both in the Authorized Version and in others also. None-
the-less, we maintain that Paul never said that the rock followed
them. In the Greek original, the objective pronoun "them"
does not occur. The clause simply reads, "That spiritual Rock
which followed," or with strict exactness, "A spiritual following
Rock." The participle—"following"—has nothing whatever to
do with following the *people*, as the context itself indicates. Paul
mentions four things which happened to the Israelites on their
vacating Egypt—

1. They all went "under the cloud"—that is, they were all
   protected by the covering "pillar of cloud";
2. They all "passed through the Sea"—and thus by the
   cloud and the sea were figuratively "baptized unto
   Moses";
3. They all did eat "the same spiritual meat" (the manna)—
   which Paul calls "spiritual" because of its miraculous and
   typical nature;
4. They all "drank of that spiritual Rock which followed"—
   that is, the smitten rock of Horeb, which was full of
   typical significance, and was thus indeed a "spiritual"
   rock.

Now these were the first four things of outstanding "spiritual"
and typical significance which happened to the Israelites on their
evacuation of Egypt. Paul mentions them in the proper order
of their occurrence; so that when he speaks of "the Rock which
followed," he is simply meaning—in accord with the actual fact
—that the rock incident followed next after the other three.

It seems almost incredible that men like Alford and Ellicott
should have missed seeing this. Yet there it is—and there can
be no doubt that this is the meaning of the Greek, logically and
grammatically, as well as being historically correct.

So there we are!—this "problem" text is really no problem
at all when we get the exact rendering and perspective of it.
The pronoun "them" is an interloper, and must be excommuni-
cated! The Rock did not follow "*them*." All that is said is that

the rock incident and the drinking of the water from it followed
the other three miracles, or "spiritual" events, which preceded it.

But before we leave this text we ought to note the inner
significance of that rock. What does that rock itself say to us?
Look at the three words once again: "*That*" . . . "*Rock*"
. . . "*Followed.*" Take the middle word first. Paul says "That
Rock was Christ." So here is clear New Testament authority for
Old Testament typology. It is by no means the only place in the
New Testament where we find such a warrant, but it is a very
definite one. In no little degree the Old Testament is permeated
by latent type-teachings. Persons, objects, events, acts, institu-
tions, are invested with prefigurative meanings, so that besides
having a real relationship with their own times they have a
significance reaching far forward into the future. In some cases
the circumstantial data are such that we could scarcely fail to
see the presence of typical correspondences even if we had no
New Testament comment to that effect. For instance, we are
nowhere told that Joseph is a type of Christ, yet who can read
that wonderful Old Testament delineation of Joseph, in the light
of New Testament history and doctrine, without perceiving in
Joseph—the beloved of his father, the rejected of his brethren,
the exalted saviour of the famine-stricken earth—one of the
fullest and clearest types of Christ anywhere in Scripture? None-
the-less, however, it is well to be clear about this, that our real
and final authority for Old Testament typology is the clear pro-
nouncement of the New Testament. "That Rock was Christ!"
(see also Rom. v. 14; Heb. vii. 3, xi. 19; 1 Pet. iii. 21, etc.).

What a regrettable thing it is that Old Testament type-teaching
is so little elucidated in the generality of modern pulpits! It is
a regrettable omission for two reasons outstandingly—(1) because
the type content of the Old Testament furnishes a grand proof
of its inspiration, being the most wonderful of all forms of *prophecy*, and (2) because it invests the Old Testament with an
endless new wealth of meaning for ourselves to-day. There seems
to be a strange ignorance even of the *presence* of such type-
teaching in the Old Testament. "Never heard such an idea before,"
said a well-known minister to a friend of mine who had preached
on one of the Old Testament types. Said another, to myself, "I
am surprised you can believe such a thing"; yet surely the far

more surprising thing is that he himself *cannot* believe it, for it is certainly there, and the New Testament again and again says so! Yes, "that Rock was Christ."

This leads to a further consideration. Take the word "that" —"*that* Rock was Christ." The typical meaning of what happened in connection with that rock of Horeb is striking indeed. See Exodus xvii. The rock itself represents Christ. Moses represents the Law. Moses was told to smite the rock (verse 6), which typifies our Lord's bearing the stroke and curse of the Law for our sakes, on Calvary. But it was not merely the hand of Moses himself which struck the rock. He was told to strike it with the "rod" (verse 5) which had now become the wonderful symbol of God's presence; and this typifies to us the fact that such is the sin of man and such is the holiness of God that the Father himself must "bruise" the sin-expiating Son. Furthermore, God said to Moses: "I will stand before thee there upon the rock" (verse 6), which strikingly adds the truth that God the Father himself suffered in the Son, that "God was in Christ, reconciling the world unto himself" (2 Cor. v. 9). It was not *until* the rock was smitten that the waters flowed forth from it; and this, of course, sets forth the *necessity* of Calvary. The living waters do not flow to us from the teaching or example of Christ merely. He must become our vicarious Sin-bearer and make atonement for us. It is from the *crucified* Saviour that the streams of salvation gush forth to mankind. And yet again, the renewing and reviving *waters* which flowed from that smitten rock typify the Holy Spirit, who is "the water of life" (see John iv. 10, 14, with vii. 39). Yes, "*that* Rock was Christ"! Wonderful Christ of Calvary!

Finally, glance again at that word, "followed." This smiting of the rock and releasing of the waters followed upon the passing "under the cloud" and "through the sea" and the eating of the manna. The people were all thus "baptized unto Moses" and made partakers together of heavenly provision. They were out of Egypt and on the way to Canaan. But did they all reach Canaan? What says Paul?—"But with many of them God was not well pleased; for they were overthrown in the wilderness." What a warning! See how Paul applies it: he says, "Wherefore, let him that thinketh he standeth take heed lest he fall." Away with presumption! We believe in the glorious doctrine of divine election and predestination—Paul himself teaches it to us; but that doctrine was meant for the comfort of genuine, honest-minded, self-denying believers on the Lord Jesus, and for no others. We simply dare not presume. On the contrary, we do well to keep Peter's exhortation ever in mind—"Wherefore the rather, brethren, give diligence to make your calling and election sure." One vital necessity in doing this is separation from the world, as Paul shows in the chapter from which our text is taken (1 Cor. x. 12–33). It is a great thing to be saved, in Christ. It is the greatest thing of all. God help us ever to keep gratefully cleaving to Christ with whole-hearted love and self-dedication to Him!

> I am saved; but is *self* buried?
>   Is my one and only aim
> Just to honour Christ my Saviour,
>   Just to glorify His name?
>
> I am saved; but am I wholly
>   *Separated* unto Him?
> Do I really shun things doubtful
>   Which my Christward vision dim?
>
> I am saved; but would I gladly
>   *Give up all*, my Lord's to be?
> If He called me, could I answer,
>   "Master, here am I, send me"?
>
> I am saved; but am I doing
>   *Everything* that I can do,
> So that souls unsaved around me
>   May be brought to Jesus too?
>
> I am saved; but is my *home* life
>   All my Lord would have it be?
> Is it seen in every action
>   That *He* has control of me?
>
> I am saved; but am I *looking*
>   For my Lord's return from heaven?
> Am I daily watching, longing
>   For the signal to be given?

MANASSEH CARRIED TO BABYLON

—2 Chronicles xxxiii. 11.

MANASSEH CARRIED TO BABYLON

"And the king of Assyria . . . took Manasseh among the thorns, and bound him with fetters, and carried him to Babylon." 2 Chronicles xxxiii. 11.

AT A FIRST glance, perhaps, there may not appear to be anything peculiar or arresting in this verse, except the sorry spectacle of Manasseh, Judah's most wicked king, now dragged away captive from Jerusalem, bound with fetters, and having "thorns," or more properly *thongs*, through his upper lip. The fact is, however, that this verse has been played as a kind of trump card against the inspiration of the Bible, by scholars of certain new schools of Biblical criticism.

The "bone of contention" is that last word in the verse—"*Babylon*." Had it been a *Babylonian* king who had taken Manasseh captive to Babylon, all would have been quite normal; but for this verse to say that a king of *Assyria*, whose capital city was *Nineveh* away on the Tigris, should carry Manasseh captive to *Babylon*, which was three hundred miles to the south, on the Euphrates—well, this is most definitely a slip, a blunder, and a clear indication that the Bible is not always reliable in its historical records!

What, then, can be said about this "problem" text? Is there a solution? Or is the Scripture chronicler wrong? The answer is that at long last evidence has turned up which proves this verse to be correct. There is now a solution to the problem, and it is as conclusive as it is interesting.

The first thing is to settle who this "king of Assyria" was, for the text leaves him unnamed. Can we identify him? We can, quite easily. Manasseh was the son of good king Hezekiah; and we know from Scripture itself that the Assyrian king who reigned contemporaneously with Hezekiah was Sennacherib (2 Kings xviii. 13; 2 Chron. xxxii). We also know, both from Scripture and from confirmatory archaeological findings, that Sennacherib was succeeded on the throne of Assyria by his son, Esarhaddon.

It would appear, also, that Manasseh had already been on the throne of Judah some years when Esarhaddon succeeded Sennacherib on the throne of Assyria—if the dates obtained from the recently disinterred Assyrian records are to be accepted. The crucial fact to note, however, is that the contemporary Assyrian king who carried Manasseh captive was *Esarhaddon.*

So the question now becomes this: Can we think that this Assyrian king, *Esarhaddon*, would carry Manasseh captive to Babylon instead of to Nineveh? The facts are as follows.

It happens that Esarhaddon had a son named Assur-bani-pal, who, when he later succeeded Esarhaddon on the throne of Assyria, collected a great library at Nineveh, including chronicles, dictionaries, medical and other writings which are now disinterred and largely deciphered. Among the many things brought to light by Assur-bani-pal's copious records of the Assyrian kings is the remarkable fact that *Esarhaddon alone of all the kings of Assyria built a palace at Babylon and lived there*!

There was a good reason for Esarhaddon's building that residence for himself at Babylon. The fact was that Babylon, despite its long subjection to Assyria, had never forgotten its former greatness when it was mistress of the vast valley between the two rivers; and during the reign of Esarhaddon's father it had showed a most dangerous restiveness. Indeed, there had broken out an open rebellion under the leadership of a certain Merodach-baladin, which had only been quelled by expensive effort on the part of the mighty Sennacherib. Therefore, when Esarhaddon came to the Assyrian throne he deemed it a wise precaution to establish his court partly at Babylon; and later in his reign he confined his rule there, handing over Nineveh and Assyria to his son, Assur-bani-pal.

Esarhaddon was thus the one monarch of Assyria who would take a captive king to *Babylon*. Sennacherib his father, and Sargon his grandfather, and Assur-bani-pal his son all lived in Nineveh, and took their captives there. Esarhaddon alone made his residence at Babylon; and the Biblical account is therefore quite in accord with the real facts when it says, in 2 Chronicles xxxiii. 11, "And the king of Assyria . . . took Manasseh among the thorns, and bound him with fetters, and carried him to Babylon." So this "problem" text is a problem no longer!

But now, this "problem" text may well be noted for further reasons which its vindication suggests. If we will let it speak to us, it will bring home to our minds certain very worth-while considerations, of which three are very relevant and important. First, our text preaches to us *the trustworthiness of Holy Scripture*. It shows us that there is good reason not to be unsettled in our minds when so-called "critical" problems are urged against the inerrancy of the Holy Scriptures. This text is by no means the only such "critical" problem which modern "scholars" have proudly played off against the older view of the Bible; nor is it by any means the only text in connection with which such presumptions on the part of Modernist religious sceptics have been exploded by the fuller information which archaeology is now supplying. The recent discoveries of archaeological explorers and decipherers in Assyria and Babylonia, following up those of Botta and Layard a hundred years ago, have thrown wonderful light on Old Testament history and ethnology. Biblical statements which have seemed contradictory or unintelligible are now shown to be quite harmonious and much to the point. With almost every new turn of the spade some new confirmation or elucidation of Scripture has been forthcoming. The solid facts now yielded up by the soil of the Orient have proved too much for the airy fancies evolved in the brains of prejudiced critics. The so-called "assured results" of the rationalist "scholars" have collapsed like houses of cards.

Certainly there are still points of difficulty, and problems yet remain; but so many have now been cleared away which at one time seemed unsolvable that it is wisdom to wait for further light which may even now be near at hand. Already the findings of archaeologists have knocked the most deadly-looking weapons out of the hand of infidelity; and the claim of the Bible to be the Word of God will yet be vindicated to the full against all who cavil or deny. Only let the next few decades bring a few more discoveries and decipherings, and the vaunted conclusions of an over-confident anti-Biblical "modern scholarship" will be for ever done away by an even *more* "modern" and far truer scholarship. Meanwhile, with such reassuring encouragement as that which we have found in connection with 2 Chronicles xxxiii. 11, let us rest confidently in the Scriptures, refusing to be shaken by the specious oppositions of Modernist "scholars" who presume to know more about Scripture history than the men who actually wrote the Scriptures.

If the Bible is really inspired of God, then its doctrines are divine, and its historical records are true. More and more its historical records are being corroborated and vindicated by fuller knowledge which the spade is bringing to us about Bible times and Bible lands. Let this fact confirm our faith in the *doctrines* of the Bible, particularly in the glad and vital doctrines of the Gospel. The facts on which the Gospel is based are real facts. The truths which are built on those facts are real truths. The salvation which the Gospel offers is a real salvation.

But second, this text preaches to us *the certainty of divine judgment upon wicked-doers*. Note that word "wherefore" at the beginning of the verse. It indicates that the calamity which befell Manasseh was in reality a direct retribution upon him for his wickedness. Who, then, meted this retribution to him? Unfalteringly the text ascribes it to God himself. Behind the insurging of the Assyrian armies was the determining hand of Jehovah. A whole volume might be written on this fact alone, for it involves one of the profoundest questions of human history and divine providence. If this verse is an inspired explanation, then no philosophy of history is true which does not take into account the sovereign hand of God controlling all events and developments.

Here, in 2 Chronicles xxxiii. 11, without any apology, is the doctrine of "poetic justice"—almighty God so ordering the affairs of nations, that exact retribution is apportioned for a particular course of wrongdoing. There are some who sit in university chairs to-day who affect scorn for the idea that God thus directly visits the sins of nations upon them. Well, if the Bible is the word of God, they are wrong. The God who punished Manasseh and Judah long ago is *still* God! He has not abdicated His throne. He has not changed in His nature. He has not slackened His control over the nations.

Those of us who believe and know the Bible to be the Word of God have been able to grasp at least something of the meaning of this in what has happened to the nations in two recent world wars. To us, indeed, those people are afflicted with a strange blindness who say they *cannot* see any evidence of supernatural control in the big anomalies of the last war. To mention only two features, was it without significance that Russia and Germany, those two great nations which had officially blasphemed God, should have been compelled, despite thier pre-war pact of friendship, to shed the blood of their sons in millions, or that Italy should have been so crushed and humiliated after her gloating savagery in Ethiopia? As truly as God overruled the revolutions of history in the days of Assyria and Babylon, so does He now in the affairs of Russia and Germany and Britain and America; and as truly as God visited the sins of nations upon them *then*, so does He *now*.

But Manasseh was an individual man, not a nation. God punishes *individuals*. Oh, we have seen sorrows and sufferings overtake men and women in such ways as left no doubt that they were being punished by an angry God for their sins. The poet, Horace, has a word to the effect that though Vengeance is lame on both feet he always overtakes his quarry in the end. God may allow a man to go to great lengths, as He did in the case of Manasseh, and as He did also in the case of Adolph Hitler, but He is never thwarted, and judgment is never dodged. Let those who presume beware! We need not think that those who evade due punishment in this present short life have finally escaped. The grave may shield a man from any other pursuer, but not from God! "If I ascend up to heaven, thou art there: if I make my bed in sheol, behold, thou art there!" As surely as divine judgment fell, at length, on Manasseh, so does it on all other evil-doers, either here or hereafter. There is absolutely no escaping the Great White Throne—except through that precious blood of Christ which is provided for the truly penitent in heart.

That leads us to a final word about our text. It reminds us of *the wonder of the divine mercy to big sinners*. See what the two verses following our text say about Manasseh: "And when he was in affliction he besought Jehovah his God, and humbled himself greatly before the God of his fathers, and prayed unto him. And God was intreated of him, and heard his supplication, and brought him again to Jerusalem into his kingdom. Then Manasseh knew that Jehovah, he was God" (verses 12 and 13). Probably Manasseh's release was granted by Esarhaddon's son,

Assur-bani-pal, who was known far and wide for his clemency to such prisoners as Manasseh.

Manasseh's repentance and restoration are a study all in themselves. See the three things that are said about his repentance—

> "He besought Jehovah" (verse 12).
> "He humbled himself greatly" (verse 12).
> "He prayed unto him" (verse 13).

And see also, in the chapter, the threefold outcome of his repentance—

> He was forgiven and restored (verse 13).
> He knew now that Jehovah was God (verse 13).
> He now lived to serve God (verses 14–20).

A certain man who had been brought up in a Christian home and had been taught the Bible got into bad company and became thoroughly worldly, and then fell into grievous sin. The lengths of sin into which he went, and the suffering and remorse which came to him afterward, drove him eventually to an almost dementing agony of concern about his soul. The more he thought about it, the more despairing he became; for it seemed to him as though he had sinned beyond redemption, especially so as he had sinned against the peculiar privileges which his Christian upbringing had given him. Then, one night, he had a remarkable dream. He found himself standing before the entrance to heaven. It was beautiful beyond anything he had ever seen before; and he could just glimpse through it some of the exquisite loveliness of heaven itself. He felt that if only he could go in there he could leave his own sinful, wretched "self" outside, and have done with it for ever; but alas, he could never enter that superbly lovely place, for the shining purity of it all made himself seem loathsomely ugly in contrast. As he watched he saw several figures come up to the entrance, and pass in. Oh, the peace and purity and radiant gladness on their faces! He heard their names: there were the Apostles John and Andrew, and several other lovely Scripture characters. How he envied them! But it was no use, he told himself; that lovely place was not for sinners like himself. Then, as he watched, others came up and went in; and among them was Mary Magdalene, out of whom, he recalled, Jesus had cast seven demons! And there, too, was Peter, who had denied his Lord with oaths and curses! And there, too, was David, who had sinned a deep and terrible sin indeed! Finally, and most astonishing of all, who should now come to that fair portal and pass in but *Manasseh*, the most wicked of all Judah's kings, but who later repented and turned to the Lord! There the dream ended, but its message was clear, and the weary, conscience-stricken dreamer found peace in the ever-open welcome of the Gospel and the cleansing blood of Calvary.

Usually we are rather suspicious of those conversions to Christ which are attributed to dreams, but we can well imagine how such a dream as that would come as a very message of God to the soul. And what a message indeed is this wicked but afterward repentant Manasseh to all sin-burdened souls, telling of the wonderful compassion and pardoning love of God! Where sin abounds grace much more abounds! None are too vile, for "the blood of Jesus Christ, God's Son, cleanseth from all sin." And Jesus says, "Him that cometh to me, I will *in no wise* cast out"!

Jesus never answered, "Nay,"
    When a sinner sought His aid;
Jesus never turned away
    When request to Him was made.
No, each weary, needy one
Found a Friend in God's dear Son.

Now upon the throne above,
    Still the self-same heart is His—
Full of tenderness and love,
    Waiting still to aid and bless.
Still may every needy one
Find a Friend in God's dear Son.

Sinner, then, to Him repair,
    Cast thy burden at His feet;
Safety, peace, and joy are there;
    Now approach His Mercy-seat.
Come, thou weary, needy one;
Find a Friend in God's dear Son!

MUST WE HATE LOVED ONES FOR CHRIST'S SAKE?

—Luke xiv. 26.

MUST WE HATE LOVED ONES FOR CHRIST'S SAKE?

"If any man come to Me, and hate not his father and mother, and wife and children, and brethren and sisters, yea, and his own life also, he cannot be My disciple; and whosoever doth not bear his cross, and come after Me, he cannot be My disciple." Luke xiv. 26.

ON ONE occasion our Lord's teaching drew from His disciples the comment, "This is an hard saying: who can hear it?" I am certain they said the same thing, at least inwardly, when He turned round on the crowd with this rebuff—"If any man come to Me, and hate not his father and mother, and wife and children, and brethren and sisters, yea, and his own life also, he cannot be My disciple." This is one of the "hard sayings" of Jesus. There never was a more gracious teacher than Jesus; nor was there ever a severer. Perhaps, if we gave more attention to His "hard sayings" the quality of our discipleship would be stauncher. The general tendency to-day is to dwell on the lighter and easier aspects of discipleship. The austerer lines are smoothed out, and Christian discipleship is made to have a velvety feel about it. This is a cheap and easy way of recruiting new converts. It brings to the Church's banners many who can shout slogans and sing choruses; but these are the sort who soon become backsliders, and who are then more difficult to reclaim than they were to be first recruited.

Our Lord himself never deceived anyone as to the real terms of discipleship. His "hard sayings" bear witness to that. He would have no man start building a tower without first counting the cost. He would have no man enter the holy war without first surveying the twenty thousand who come against him. He would have no man don the livery of the Gospel without taking into account the fiery baptism with which he must be baptized. He would have no man set out for the heavenly crown without duly considering the cross which must be shouldered. It is well, then, that we should review our Lord's "hard sayings," and keep close to His example, lest our discipleship degenerates into a loosely-held outward profession, instead of a passionate, resolute, sacrificial separation to Him from the ways of "this present evil world."

I have just looked again through our Lord's pronouncements on this matter of discipleship, and in my own judgment the severest thing He ever said is that which is recorded in our text —"If any man come to Me, and hate not his father and mother, and wife and children, and brethren and sisters, yea, and his own life also, he cannot be My disciple." It pierces us at our most sensitive nerve—parents, wife, children. Nor is that all; there is a *problem* here which stings us like a nettle, in that word, "hate" —"If any man *hate* not his father and mother . . ." Did our Lord really mean that our attachment of love to Himself, on the one hand, must involve a detachment of hate, on the other, from our earthly kith and kin? Or is there some less severe way of taking the words? Yet if there *is* a smoother meaning, why did our Lord *use* that word "hate"? Why did He not make His real intention clearer on such a tender issue? We are all conscious of the problem here; and we find it evoking two main questions—(1) What do the words really mean? (2) How do they bear on ourselves to-day?

WHAT DO THE WORDS REALLY MEAN?

First, then, *what do the words really mean?* We can best arrive at the true answer by preliminarily settling how the words are *not* to be taken. And to begin with, let us be quite clear that they are not to be taken *literally*. That may sound too bluntly final, but it is true. It is a sound, basic principle of Biblical exegesis that wherever the words of Scripture can be taken literally they should be taken so. It is a principle to which we ourselves constantly adhere. But our Lord's words here, about hating one's father, mother, wife, children, brethren, simply cannot be taken literally, or they would flatly contradict His own teaching and His own example, quite apart from contradicting the fifth commandment and the general teaching of Holy Writ. The words are no more to be taken literally than those other words of Christ—"I came not to send peace, but a sword," "I am come to send fire on earth," "I am come to set a man at variance against his father." No, the words are not to be taken literally.

Nor are they to be taken *comparatively*, though this is the usual explanation. Look up the well-known expositors, and you will find that almost uniformly they explain our Lord's words here as meaning that we are to love Him so intensely that *in comparison* our love for others, even our nearest and dearest, is to be as hate. They may not all put it so baldly as that, but that is the drift of their comment. Yet the more one considers it, the less acceptable does this explanation become; for the fact is that the more truly and deeply we love our Lord, the more really and devotedly we love our earthly kith and kin. Remember, the words were spoken to a crowd, many of whom were genuinely seeking, but none of whom knew Christ closely. They had not lived with Him night and day, and been able thereby to fall in love with His stainless, beautiful character; nor were they going to have that opportunity afterward. If, therefore, they were to wait until their love for Him was so fervent that all other loves were comparatively hate, they could never have become His disciples at all! I am speaking what is true of many when I speak of my own conversion: I really believed on Christ for salvation. I had the inward assurance that I was now a true disciple of the Lord Jesus. Yet I scarcely knew Him then by personal fellowship; and my love for Him certainly was not such that in comparison all other loves were hatreds. Yet did Jesus say of me, "He cannot be My disciple"? No! And if there is a sin-burdened seeker now following my words, I would say, "Wait not until your love for Christ has grown into an intense fire: trust Him this minute; and He will in no wise cast you out." Christian discipleship moves in progressive stages. We begin as *believers*, then become *servants*, and then *friends*, and then *lovers*.

But if our Lord's words here are not to be taken either literally or comparatively, what then? They are to be taken *ostensibly*. There are two key-expressions in the text which explain this—

(1) the phrase, "Yea, and his own life also";
(2) the clause, "Whosoever doth not bear his cross."

Take the first of these. Our Lord says that a man cannot be His disciple unless he hates *"his own life also."* Now for a man to hate his own life (literally, "his own soul") is a patent impossibility. I know that at times some of us may have exclaimed, "Oh, I hate myself!" but that expression simply means that we are displeased at something we have done, or at certain ways to which we are addicted. I simply cannot hate my own soul without being an irrational self-contradiction. Does someone say: Surely the suicide is a man who hates his own life? Wrong! Suicide is either the product of mental unsoundness or else it is a form of self-consideration—an attempt to escape, to save oneself from threatening circumstances. If the suicide's circumstances were only what he wishes they were, he would not take his life. Suicide is really self-consideration resorting to the drastic extreme. No, our Lord's words about a man's hating "his own life also" simply cannot be taken either literally or comparatively—and this confirms that the hating of father, mother, wife, children, brothers, sisters, must not be taken literally or comparatively either.

Now look at the clause, *"Whosoever doth not bear his cross . . ."* We need to remember that these words were spoken before our Lord went to the cross of Calvary. None of His thronging hearers knew that He would yet be nailed to a cross, though He himself knew, and had already mentioned it to the inner ring of His disciples (Luke ix. 22, 23); but as soon as He used that word "cross" their ears would be startled. As soon as He said, "Whosoever does not bear his *cross*, and come after Me, cannot be My disciple," they would start back, for a cross meant three things—shame, suffering, death, all of the worst kind. What! Did being His disciple mean *that*? Yes, it did. Our Lord knew well enough that thousands of those who became His disciples in those early days would become *martyrs*. He knew that by becoming a Christian many a man would put himself into a position in which it would *seem* as though he hated his nearest and dearest. It would mean shame, suffering, and death; and if a man deliberately chose to be His disciple, with such consequences in view, it would verily *seem* to his loved ones as though he hated them, as though he were deliberately wronging them, courting death, and hating his own life.

Try to get into the circumstances of many a Christian in those martyr days. The officers of the crown have come to a hitherto happy home, to arrest the father on a charge of allegiance to the illegal sect of the Nazarene. He can utter an oath of disavowal there and then which will absolve him; otherwise he must be condemned and committed to the beasts on the floor of the Colosseum or some other arena. Which shall it be—denial of Christ, or seeming hate of loved ones? The man's distraught wife flings her arms round him and pleads with sobs, for her own sake and the children's sake. The little ones, with their bonny faces but frightened looks and appealing eyes, cling about him. The man's own parents appear on the scene, with every tender, urgent argument to dissuade him from his attachment to the despised Nazarene heresy. How dare he be so cruel to his faithful wife and dependent bairns? It is all so needless. One word from him, and all will be well. See how the wife sinks down overcome! See how the children sob! See how the neighbours all concur! The great God in heaven never meant such a mad course for any man. Such cruelty to loved ones simply cannot be right. And after all, who *was* this Jesus?—a peasant, a Jew, a nobody; nay, worse, a deceiver, a crucified criminal, executed by the demand of His own people! But the Christian man refuses to forswear his loyalty. He allows himself to be led away by the officers—to shame and suffering and ignominious death. The neighbourhood pronounces it monstrous. To all appearance it would seem as though his attachment to the crucified Nazarene had turned the natural love in him to hate—else how could he be so unfaithful to his father and mother and wife and children and brothers and sisters?

That is what our Lord had in mind when He said, "If any man come to Me, and hate not his father and mother, and wife and children, and brethren and sisters, yea, and his own life also, he cannot be My disciple; and whosoever doth not bear his cross, and come after Me, he cannot be My disciple." He never meant that becoming His disciple would make a man hate his own kith and kin in actual *fact*; but only *ostensibly*, that is, *in outward seeming only*.

So, then, to sum up this aspect of the matter, this problematical paradox of Jesus about hating one's own loved ones does not mean hate either literally or comparatively, but only ostensibly, or apparently, or merely in outward seeming. *It has to do with special circumstances.*

Therefore, instead of thinking that *we* to-day are to hate our own families, and instead of vexing our minds even as to whether we love Christ so intensely that all other loves are hatreds in comparison, let us realise that our Lord's words have no such implication, and let us thank God that those times of anti-Christian persecution which called forth our Lord's words are no longer with us, at least among the English-speaking peoples, forcing us into situations such as the early Christians were forced into, of even *seeming* to hate our nearest and dearest. With many of us to-day, to be Christ's means that instead of even *seeming* to hate our kith and kin we give them cause for gratitude to God on our behalf.

I am not unmindful, of course, that even to-day conversion to Christ sometimes brings painful estrangements in families. Am I not right, indeed, in assuming that some whom I now address know something of this in all-too-sorrowful experience? Speaking generally, however, the circumstances to-day do not force us into such situations of seeming hate to loved ones as the early Christians were forced into; and for this we may well be most deeply grateful to God.

HOW DO THE WORDS BEAR ON OURSELVES TO-DAY?

We come now to our second question: How do these words of our Lord really bear on ourselves to-day? Read the words carefully again: "If any man come to Me, and hate not his father and mother, and wife and children, and brethren and sisters, yea, and his own life also, he cannot be My disciple; and whosoever doth not bear his cross, and come after Me, he cannot be My disciple."

While these words do not mean that we must hate our nearest and dearest, either literally or comparatively, they certainly do mean that *in every crisis of choice Christ must come first.* Christians should love the members of their families with a purer and more considerate love than do others. Christian sons and daughters should love their parents with a really dutiful and obvious love.

Christian husbands and wives, brothers and sisters, should love their own all the more genuinely and practically because of their new allegiance to Christ. Yet in any real crisis which is forced upon us, in which we are compelled to choose between Christ and others, Christ must come first. I have been in public work long enough now to know that however careful one may be, the most carefully worded utterance may be picked up the wrong way, and I tremble lest I should be misunderstood on *this* most delicate point of the Christian's relationship toward relatives. There are some professing Christians who *aggravate* opposition to themselves, and then think they are heroes for Christ's sake because they suffer! There are other Christians who seem needlessly to irritate the other members of their households, and then attribute the estrangement to their Christian faith instead of to their provocative awkwardness! Beware; it is not an essential part of Christian profession to quarrel with relatives! But when through no fault of our own, except our attachment to Christ, we are forced to a painful choice, Christ must come first.

That leads to a further thought. If in every such choice Christ must come first, then it means that we must *love* Christ most. Yes, our text cannot mean less than that: *Christ must be first in the love of our hearts.* This is corroborated by the parallel passage in Matthew x. 37, 38—"He that loveth father or mother *more than Me* is not worthy of Me; and he that loveth son or daughter *more than Me* is not worthy of Me. . . ." Experience shows that only too often the greatest foes of a man's soul are those who are nearest and dearest to him by natural ties. In most cases they *do not mean* to do him harm, and they *do not know* that they are going against his highest interests; they just do not understand. When he becomes concerned about the salvation of his soul, they tell him that he is becoming unduly worried, that he ought not to take such religious matters too seriously, that he is quite as good as lots who profess Christianity, and that surely God never meant us to be oddities, and so on. No, they just do not understand. Sometimes the greatest of all hindrances in the conversion of men and women to Christ is this discouragement at home. If conversion actually takes place, then this misunderstanding and discouragement sometimes develops into deliberate opposition; a collision of beliefs and opinions then takes place; and the Christian is forced to make choice between offending Christ and offending those who are dearest on earth. It is a painful situation to be in. We should avoid it as far as is consistently possible. But if such a situation *does* arise, we must put Christ first, whatever the cost. This being misunderstood by our loved ones and friends is the special "cross" which our Lord forewarned us we would have to bear (Matt. x. 38). It will certainly be a "cross" if we greatly love those whom we have to offend, or to suffer from, for Christ's sake; but our love for our dear Lord must be supreme.

This leads to still another reflection. In view of our Lord's words, *we should carefully review our discipleship*. Indeed, our Lord quite evidently *meant* that His words should cause His hearers thus to pause and consider: see the verses immediately following—"For which of you, intending to build a tower, sitteth not down first and counteth the cost, whether he have sufficient to finish it? . . . Or what king, going to make war with another king, sitteth not down first and consulteth whether he be able with ten thousand to meet him that cometh against him with twenty thousand? . . ." Away with cheap and easy notions of the Christian life! It costs something to be a real Christian; and our Lord says, "Count the cost!" To be a merely nominal Christian, simply attending services and meetings and social functions, may be cheap and easy work; but to follow Christ closely, to confess Him in whatever company we find ourselves, to live a life of real self-denial, to renounce our dearest sins and our most excusable self-justification and all indulgent ease and worldliness—well, *that* sort of a Christian life *does* cost (and it is the only Christian life which really *tells* and really *pays* in the end).

When our Lord uttered the words of our text and of the verses which follow it, He was addressing the multitude, and His purpose was to weed out the unreal from the real among His followers. He wanted quality in preference to quantity. He wanted no arm-chair soldiers in His army. He therefore let the crowd know in advance the risks and costs of discipleship. But perhaps some ease-loving disciple of to-day says, "Well, anyway, I've been converted; I'm a saved soul; that's the main thing; and so far as other things are concerned I'm no laxer than lots of other professing Christians." Yes, friend, it is true that by simple faith in the Lamb of Calvary you are saved (if it be a *true* faith); you are saved from the "second death" and the fire of Gehenna; but do you think you will share the rewards and glories of those who have loved and served Christ with an out-and-out loyalty? You know the answer.

See the stern warning with which our Lord ends His word on discipleship and counting the cost. He says: "So likewise, whosoever he be of you that forsaketh not all that he hath, he cannot be My disciple. Salt is good; but if the salt have lost his savour, wherewith shall it be seasoned? It is neither fit for the land, nor yet for the dunghill; but men cast it out. He that hath ears to hear, let him hear" (Luke xiv. 33–5). The disciple who starts out without duly counting the cost and then becomes a backslider is compared to salt gone bad! No man is in such a dangerous state as one who has once known the truth and has professed to love it, and then fallen away. You can tell him nothing he does not already know. He has not sinned against an unknown God. He has gone away from Christ with his eyes open. His case is well nigh desperate.

Oh, it is well worth while at last to have been out-and-out for Christ, to have put Him first in our love and life, and to have counted all things as nothing compared with the excellency of knowing Him as our Saviour. It is then that we can pass beyond with Paul's martyrdom exclamation on our lips—

"I have fought the good fight; I have finished the course; I have kept the faith. Henceforth there is laid up for me A CROWN OF RIGHTEOUSNESS, which the Lord, the righteous judge, shall give me at that day: and not to me only, but unto all them also that love His appearing!"

Setting out to liberate Italy, Garibaldi saw a group of young fellows at a street corner, and summoned them to rally to him. "What do you offer?" they asked. "Offer?" replied Garibaldi. "I offer you hardship, hunger, rags, thirst, sleepless nights, foot-sores in long marches, privations innumerable; and victory in the noblest cause that ever asked you." Young Italy followed him. So is it in the holy war to which Christian discipleship commits us. Our Lord never hid the cross which would have to be borne by us. When you come to think of it, in Christian life and service there is nothing which really counts that does not really cost. The way of salvation is easy; but the Christian life is hard, for the "flesh" contests every step of spiritual progress. The gifts of the Gospel and the graces of the Spirit are free; but real discipleship always costs, for the "self" in us resists long and desperately. Yes, this side of heaven, and under present circumstances, there are costs. There is a price to pay—

> For the joy set before thee,
>> The cross;
> For the gain that comes after,
>> The loss;
> For the morning that smileth,
>> The night;
> For the peace of the victor,
>> The fight.
>
> For the white rose of goodness,
>> The thorn;
> For the Spirit's deep wisdom,
>> Men's scorn;
> For the sunshine of gladness,
>> The rain;
> For the fruit of God's pruning,
>> The pain.
>
> For the clear bell of triumph,
>> The knell;
> For the sweetness of meeting,
>> Farewell;
> For the height of the mountain,
>> The steep;
> For the waking in heaven,
>> Death's sleep.

Yes, there is a price to pay; but in the end the cross gives place to the crown, and the world's frown to the heavenly King's "Well done!" God help us to love our earthly kin with a pure and tender affection, yet to put Christ absolutely first, and gladly pay each price for His dear sake.

Oh, the rapture at last, Lord,
> For me;
Oh, the infinite sweetness—
> With Thee!
Help me gladly each price, Lord,
> To pay,
For the bliss all-excelling,
> That day.

NO SCRIPTURE OF
"PRIVATE INTERPRETATION"?
—2 Peter i. 20.

NO SCRIPTURE OF
"PRIVATE INTERPRETATION"?

*"Knowing this first, that no prophecy of the Scripture is of
any private interpretation . . ."* 2 Peter i. 20.

THERE were three fundamental propositions for which the
Protestant reformers battled in the sixteenth century, and on
which ground they won the glorious victory of the Reformation.
These were (1) the supremacy and sufficiency of the Holy Scriptures, (2) the right and duty of private judgment, (3) justification
by faith alone, apart from deeds of the Law, penances of the
Church, or supposed human merit-works of any sort. May God
keep us immovably grounded there! These three principles are
being assailed with renewed energy and much subtlety to-day.
We must defend them with a corresponding tenacity. "Keep
firm hold of them (of these three basic doctrines) when you
argue with a Roman Catholic," says J. C. Ryle, in his forthright,
vigorous style, "and your position is unassailable. Give up any
one of them, and your cause is lost. Like Samson with his hair
shorn, your strength is gone. Like the Spartans, betrayed at
Thermopylae, you are out-flanked and surrounded. You cannot maintain your ground. Resistance is useless."

Just here, we pick on the second of these three vital Protestant
tenets—*the right and duty of private interpretation* in relation to
the Holy Scriptures and matters of the Christian faith. The
Roman Church demands *implicit faith*, that is, you are to believe
and obey what the Church says, in any given matter, whether
you yourself understand why or not. The authority of the Church
overrides your individual reasoning-power. You are to believe
implicitly what the Church teaches, and subordinate your own
private judgment. How intelligent and educated people to-day
can sell their souls and surrender their intellects to such a system
of pseudo-religious Hitlerism, especially with the background of
Rome's history and influence in view, is an enigma to ourselves;
but this is precisely what they do.

59

Protestantism, on the other hand, stands for *explicit* faith; that is, without coercion it asks every man to make a free and intelligent choice, honouring his own conscience and responsibility, with all the facts before him. It claims for every man the right of access to the Holy Scriptures, and the right of private judgment in relation to those Scriptures. It says that if the Holy Scriptures are indeed the written word of God, then no church or ecclesiastical body on earth has the right to veto a man's independent reading of them, or to violate his liberty of conscience and exercise of free judgment before God. In the words of 1 Thessalonians v. 21, Protestantism says to every man, "Prove all things; hold fast that which is good."

But what, then, about 2 Peter i. 20—"Knowing this first, that no prophecy of the Scripture is of any private interpretation"? Does not this run counter to the Protestant principle of "private judgment"? The Roman Church would certainly like us to think so. Down through the years she has traded much on the obscurity which has somehow clung round this text. Her theologians have taken advantage of our English translation of the verse to bolster up their apologetic that Scripture is only to be interpreted by their church, not by private individuals. And we have met many Protestant people who, even to-day, seem shaky as to what this verse means. What, then, does 2 Peter i. 20 really tell us?

Well, we are glad to say that this is a case where careful reference to the *wording*, to the *context*, and to the *scope of the passage*, settles the meaning beyond the shadow of a doubt.

First, then, what of these two words, "private" and "interpretation"? The Greek word translated as "private" is *idios*, which occurs 114 times in the New Testament, and is almost always translated as meaning that which is *one's own*—"his own sheep," "his own country," "his own servants"; but never once outside 2 Peter i. 20 is it translated by the word "private." So the rendering of it as "private" in our problem-text is certainly irregular.

The other Greek word, translated as "interpretation," is *epilusis*. It occurs nowhere else in the New Testament, but its verb form, *epiluo*, comes in Mark iv. 34 and Acts xix. 39, where it is translated as "expound" and "determined." This guides us. The verb means to *let loose* or *break open* or *unfold*, as in "expounding" or "making known,"—see Acts xix. 39.

If we now return, with this gathered information, to 2 Peter i. 20, and translate more precisely, we shall change the word "private" to "*its own*," and "interpretation" to "*unfolding*" or "*breaking forth*." Moreover, the little word "is" in this text represents the Greek *ginomai*, which means to *become*, or to come into being. Therefore, translating more strictly, we get—

"*No prophecy of Scripture springs (or comes into being) of its own unfolding (or by self-origination).*"

Careful examination of the wording, therefore, shows, or at least *seems* to show, that Peter's real thought here has to do, not with the "interpretation" of Scripture, but with its *origination*.

Now, secondly, we must inspect the *context*. Does this support our emended reading of the verse? It does. The verse which follows our text begins with the connective, "for," showing that it closely continues the thought. And it says, "For no prophecy was ever brought forth by the will of man, but men spake from God, being moved by the Holy Spirit" (A.S.V. marg.). Here again, as plainly as can be, it is not the "*interpretation*" but the *origination* of Scripture which is in mind.

And, thirdly, we must refer to the *scope of the whole passage*. What is the subject treated of? Well, see verses 16 to 21.

A.—APOSTOLIC WITNESS (verses 16–18).

  (1) What it was *not* (verse 16).
      Not "cunningly devised" (or self-originated) myths.
  (2) What it *is* (verse 19).
      First-hand witness of the Lord's "power and coming."
  (3) How it *came* (verses 17, 18).
      "Voice from excellent glory"; "Voice from heaven."

B.—PROPHETIC WITNESS (verses 19–21).

  (1) What it is *not* (verse 20).
      Not of its own unfolding (i.e., not of self-origination).
  (2) And what it *is* (verse 19).
      "A light that shineth in a dark place, until the day dawn."
  (3) And how it *came* (verse 21).
      "Men spake from God, being moved by the Holy Spirit."

Surely, that finally settles it. Peter's subject is the apostolic and prophetic witness—how it did *not* originate, and how it *did* originate. The subject is not the "interpretation" of Scripture at all, but the origination of it; *not* what the Scripture *means*, but *whence it came*. This at once brushes clean away from our text the cute little webs which sly old spiders from Rome have spun round it.

And so we come back with renewed conviction to our sound old Protestant principle, namely, *the right and duty of private interpretation.* God help us to prize and guard this right, and to exercise our conscience to godliness by the daily reading of His written word!

A PRESENT PERIL

It is certainly timely, just now, to think and speak about this right and duty of private judgment; for this vital, Protestant principle is being jeopardised to-day as never before since the Reformation. It is being attacked everywhere by two determined forms of totalitarianism—the totalitarian *State* of Communism, and the totalitarian *Church* of Romanism. These two are bent on obliterating our hard-won Protestant liberties.

There is a rather grim comfort, perhaps, in the fact that the totalitarian State, as represented by Moscow, and the totalitarian Church, as represented by Rome, are undisguised enemies of each other. None the less, they are both the sworn foes of Protestant, evangelical, New Testament Christianity; for New Testament Christianity is essentially democratic (and, let us never forget, it is the influence of the New Testament which lies behind the democracy of the greatest two democratic groups today, the British and the North American!). Our prayer is that Communism and Romanism may destroy each other. Possibly they will, though the whole earth will bleed in the struggle. May they never become friends, this modern Pilate and Herod, in crucifying afresh the Lord of glory!

Meanwhile, our precious, vital, Protestant principle of the right and duty of private judgment is in acute peril. Our educational and economic system to-day tends to betray us either to Romanism or to Communism. We are more and more doting on specialisation in the various branches of art and science, of culture and polity. There are the specialists in this line and that line and the other line; and the tendency is to say, on any given matter, "Oh, leave that to the experts." Now that is wrong, fatally wrong. And especially is it so in the realm of spiritual concerns.

Again and again, recently, I myself have come up against this attitude of mind, when talking to people about their spiritual interests. "Oh, I leave religious matters to be decided for me by the specialists in those concerns: I have not the time or the knowledge to go into those things on my own." Such an attitude, I repeat, is utterly fatal. Quite apart from the fact that the experts are often wrong, and apart from the fact that specialists are notoriously unreliable when it comes to assessing the value of general evidence, to shuffle so lazily out of responsible thinking on the most sacred and basic things of life is simply to yell for a return of slavery in some form or another. If the individual stops thinking for himself on those matters which most. concern the preservation of man's true dignity, then others will pretty quickly begin to do his thinking for him. The totalitarian State or the totalitarian Church will toss away his independence, and shackle him with evils which will make him think for himself when it is too late!

It is for such reasons that a revival of Protestant, evangelical Christianity would be the greatest blessing that could come to nation and people just now. It would bring a revival of individual thinking about the supreme things, about the things which determine progress or decline in all the other spheres of human life. It would revive our estimate of the value of the individual, which Romanism, Communism, and the baneful (and altogether unproven) doctrine of Evolution all tend to diminish. We are desperately needing such a revival. We are needing a revival of individual thinking about God, the soul, ultimate destiny, and the inviolable sanctity, value, and responsibility of the individual human being, as made "in the image of God."

Now what are the basic reasons for this vital Protestant principle? There are three sets of reasons. First, there are reasons in the Scriptures themselves. Second, there are reasons in our constitution as human beings. Third, there are reasons historical, political, civil.

REASONS IN THE SCRIPTURES

We say there are reasons in the Scriptures themselves: and there are. To begin with, the *language* of the Bible is understandable by the individual. Admittedly, there are some things "hard to be understood" in the Scriptures; but these are just as hard to be understood by councils as individuals, for they are mainly dispensational matters, or prophecies which the Spirit of inspiration has designedly made enigmatical until their fulfilment in history. Speaking generally, the Bible is of all books the plainest. It is intelligible to all who can read.

Further, the Scriptures are everywhere *addressed* to the individual, that is, they are addressed to men in general, as responsible beings, or to the whole body of Christian believers as such, without the slightest suggestion of need for any intermediary interpreter of any kind whatever.

And again, the Scriptures actually *enjoin* private judgment. See John v. 39. Our Lord Himself says, "Search the Scriptures." He was addressing the Jews indiscriminately; and He quite clearly assumed that they were able to understand what the Old Testament had said about the coming Christ, even though its predictions had been misunderstood by the Elders and Scribes and the whole Sanhedrin! Or turn to Galatians i. 8, 9, where Paul says: "But though we or an angel from heaven preach any other gospel unto you than that which we have preached unto you, let him be accursed." Note the implication: these Galatian believers had the right to sit in judgment even on an apostle or an angel, because they had an infallible rule by which their judgment of any doctrine was to be determined, namely, a previously authenticated revelation of God. If, then, Scripture recognises the right of the people to judge the teachings even of apostles and angels, how much more have they the right to judge the doctrines of bishops and priests!

REASONS IN HUMAN NATURE

In our very constitution as human beings, there are arguments for this principle of the right and duty of private judgment in relation to the Scriptures and the Christian faith. First, there are innate *obligations* for us to exercise this right and duty. We are beings possessing intellect, conscience, free-will; and we are therefore accountable to God. And if each must answer for himself, each must *judge* for himself.

Second, there are also within us the *provisions* for the exercise of this right and duty. Possessing intellect, we have the power to discriminate between truth and error. Possessing conscience, we have the faculty to discriminate between right and wrong. Possessing free-will, we have the prerogrative of *choice* between truth and error, and between right and wrong. With the inspired Scriptures in our hands, and these faculties of discretion and decision constitutionally within us, there are both the obligations and the provisions for the exercise of this right and duty of private judgment.

Third, there is the gift of *the Holy Spirit*, who not only regenerates, but illuminates all who become savingly united to Christ. Is the Holy Spirit given as guide and teacher only to apostles, councils, clerics? No! He is given to all the elect of God in Christ. See Acts ii. 38, 39; Romans viii. 9, 16; 1 Corinthians xii. 7, 13; Ephesians i. 13, 14, 17; 1 John ii. 20, 27, and other such verses. To deny believers the right of private judgment, therefore, is to deny the Holy Spirit his ministry and to come about as near to committing the unpardonable sin as anything we know. Yet the Roman Church arrogates this prerogative to herself, and would force upon us an external, stereotyped interpretation which has been decided upon by cardinals and councils and made final by papal seal. God forbid!

REASONS HISTORICAL AND CIVIL

Finally, there are reasons historical and civil for preserving his healthful Protestant tenet of the right and duty of private interpretation. Nowhere, either in New Testament history or in subsequent history is there any evidence or the slightest indication that our Lord or His apostles ever transferred this right and duty from the individual to the organised Church. The claim of the Roman Church is as gratuitous, therefore, in this connection as is her claim of apostolical succession.

Moreover, throughout history, those who have drawn their religion directly from the Scriptures, by the exercise of private interpretation have shown a general unity as to essential faith and practice—a unity with so few exceptions, and with the exceptions so clearly answered, that the exceptions have proved the rule. There has been no need whatever for any hard and fast ecclesiastically authorised and regulated interpretation, imposed by some central body.

And again, everywhere, from New Testament days until now, the exercise of the right and duty of private judgment in relation to the Scriptures and the Christian faith has been productive of moral and social improvement. The denial of this right has had the very opposite effect. Look at South America. Look at Spain. Look at Eire. Look at Italy. We despise the Roman emperor Nero as a madman or a monster for fooling about on his guitar while Rome was burning; but in truth he was no more stupid than those thousands of men and women to-day, who are supinely allowing this precious, vital right of free, individual judgment to slip from them into the hands of the totalitarian Church or the totalitarian State. A central monopoly, either in religion or in politics, is ultimately fatal to the real progress of any nation or people. Human dictatorship, either in politics or in morals, was never meant for beings made in the image of God!

If the Scriptures are indeed the inspired word of God, the divine rule of faith and practice, and if the eternal destiny of men and women is determined by their response thereto, then it follows that if any set of men can seize the exclusive right to interpret the Scriptures, they can impose whatever conditions of salvation they see fit; and thus, having the salvation of the people in their hands, they become absolute masters. This is exactly what the Roman church has done, and established thereby a tyranny which has no parallel in history. Nor is it to be wondered at that wherever Rome has gained the upper hand, not only has religious liberty disappeared, but political and civil liberty also.

Without a doubt, the right and duty of private judgment is absolutely vital as a safeguard of both civil and religious liberty and progress. God save us from both those totalitarianisms which would destroy this precious Protestant principle to-day! God save us from Communism! God save us from Romanism!

"WHOSE SOEVER SINS YE REMIT"

—John xx. 23.

"WHOSE SOEVER SINS YE REMIT"

*"Whose soever sins ye remit, they are remitted unto them;
and whose soever sins ye retain, they are retained."*
John xx. 23.

NOT LONG ago we received a letter from a young soldier in which
he told us of a discussion between himself and a Roman Catholic.
He had more than held his own until the Roman Catholic quoted
the above text, claiming that it conferred upon Roman Catholic
priests the authority to grant absolution from sin. Our young
friend was "quite stumped" (as his letter put it), and did not
know what to reply.

The Romanists certainly have exploited this text, and we have
no doubt that many Protestant believers have been perplexed
by it. What then does it really signify? In reply we would say
that there are two factors which, when duly considered, lead us
quite conclusively to the true interpretation—(1) the *persons* to
whom the words were spoken, (2) the *time* when the words were
spoken.

First, then, as to *the persons to whom the words were addressed*:
either the words were spoken to our Lord's disciples in general,
or to ten of the Apostles in particular. The context simply calls
them "disciples." If the words were meant for disciples in
general, they simply cannot mean to confer some special power
on any particular *class* of disciples, much less on the Romanist
priest-class which did not come into being until some centuries
later. If the words were spoken to disciples in general, then
whatever else this verse may or may not teach, we can only
say that for Roman priests to claim it as teaching a peculiar
prerogative conferred upon *them* is as preposterous as any of the
preposterous claims which their church ever made.

If, on the other hand, the words were spoken, not to the
disciples in general, but to the Apostles in particular, the Roman
priests are just as badly off, if not worse. Were the Apostles
priests? NO. They were plain, working men. Did they ever

become priests? ˙ NO. Did they ever *ordain* priests? NO. The New Testament knows absolutely nothing of any order of priesthood in the Christian Church except the priesthood of all believers (see 1 Pet. ii. 5, 9; Rev. i. 6, etc.). No Roman Catholic can contradict this. So, then, if John xx. 23 was spoken exclusively to the *Apostles* it certainly gives nothing to Roman *priests*!

As for the claim of the Roman Church that her priesthood is *derived* from the Apostles, and that the authority to absolve from sin is thus *transmitted* by "Apostolical succession," well, quite apart from the refutation of this implied in what we have just said, the whole idea of "Apostolical succession" is a figment. There are big historical gaps in the supposed succession, which none can ever piece together; and besides this, the so-called "laying on of hands" by bishops (in whom the succession is supposed to run) is equally ridiculous in this connection, for in the New Testament it is not just Apostles or other public officials in the churches who lay their hands on other believers, but all the believers in common! (see Acts xiii. 3).

So there we are. Whether the words of our text were spoken to the "disciples" generally or to the "Apostles" exclusively, there is certainly not a vestige of any warrant here for the (pretended) absolution of penitents by Romanist priests.

But now note the *time* when the words were spoken. It was before ever the Church had come into historical existence. This at once cautions us. There is no mention of the Church in the context. This further cautions us. The fact is, the words do not refer to the Church at all, but to the "Kingdom of Heaven." One of the major blunders of the Roman Church is its confusion of the "Church" and the "Kingdom". We see this in the case of Matthew xvi. 19, on the basis of which Rome says that our Lord gave the keys of the Church to Peter. Our Lord did no such thing. He said: "I will give unto thee the keys of *the kingdom of heaven*."

So here, in John xx. 23, the words refer to the Kingdom, not to the Church. If they referred by anticipation to the Church which was yet to come into being, then *most certainly* they would reappear, in doctrinal form, in that part of Holy Scripture which is specifically written *to* and *about* the Church and its ministers —that is, the Christian Church Epistles (Romans to 2 Thessalonians) and the Pastoral Epistles (1 Timothy to Philemon).

But what do we find in those Epistles? There is absolutely no mention of any separate priest-class; nor is there any mention of "bishops" in the modern sense of that word; nor is there a solitary mention of any such remission of sins even by Apostles; nor is there any such mention in any other Epistle of the New Testament.

But what do we mean when we say that the words of John xx. 23 refer to the Kingdom of Heaven? We will try to explain very briefly. The main message of our Lord's preaching was the offer of "The Kingdom of Heaven." This was the kingdom fore-promised in the Old Testament Scriptures. The Jewish people, however, had so doted on the outward and material aspects of that kingdom that they were ill-disposed toward its ethical and spiritual requirements. Our Lord's message was rejected, and the King Himself was crucified. Yet on the Cross our Lord uttered a deeply significant word—"Father, forgive them, for they know not what they do"; and in consequence of this, the nation Israel was given a renewed opportunity to receive its Messiah-King and the Kingdom of Heaven. This renewed opportunity was given during the period covered by the Book of the Acts of the Apostles.

The thirty years or so covered by the Book of the Acts were a suspense-period. Had the nation repented and responded, the Lord Jesus would thereupon have returned (Acts iii. 20). The miraculous "signs" of those Pentecostal days were the God-given evidences that the Kingdom was indeed being offered again to the nation. But the nation again refused, and the miracle-signs were correspondingly withdrawn. It was only as the further Jewish rejection of the Lord Jesus became more and more fixed that God's further movement in history, through the Church, was made known (see Eph. iii. 3–10).

Now the "Apostles" were a group of men in a category all by themselves. They were men specially endowed with mira-culous gifts and supernatural prerogatives for a special purpose in a special time. This fact has a direct bearing on our text. We can see now that our Lord's words do not refer to the "Church" at all, and certainly not to any ecclesiastical priest-class: they refer to those specially endowed men and to the special period covered by the Acts of the Apostles, in which the renewed offer of the Kingdom was made to Israel. We say again that the "Apostles" were a group of men in a category all by themselves, belonging to a special epoch. They were never *meant* to have "successors"! The New Testament nowhere promises that they *would* have successors. Nor have they ever *had* successors in the way that Rome pretends. When the Apostles died, the special prerogatives of that Apostolic age died with them; and they will not reappear until the King Himself reappears in the glory of His second advent, to set up at last the long-deferred kingdom.

We wish we had more space here to develop all this; but we have at least said enough to indicate what we believe is the true reference of the text.

Perhaps we ought just to add that quite apart from any dispensational consideration such as we have just mentioned, there are other cogent considerations which help to determine the true purport of our Lord's words in John xx. 23.

First, we note that the prerogative to remit or to retain sins was given in conjunction with a special enduement of the Holy Spirit (verse 22), and without the remotest possible reference to any such ecclesiastical *office* as that of a priest. Whatever this remission or retention of sins meant, it was not something to be handed down by succession in *office*, but something which had to do with *a direct infilling of the Holy Spirit himself*—and we know that this infilling was certainly not restricted to the Apostles, nor has it ever since been restricted to any one class in the Church, much less to Roman priests!

Second, whatever the words may have meant, the disciples to whom they were spoken evidently never understood that they themselves were thereby empowered to become absolving priests. If the word "disciples" in verses 19 and 20 means the disciples generally, men and women included, then *they* certainly never so understood the words. But it would seem, also, that even the Apostles were never aware of having any such power, for there is no record anywhere that they ever exercised it. They were utterly innocent of being priests after the Romanish type. They did not exercise any such priestly function at all. They preached the Gospel, and, as our Lord's witnesses, declared the forgiveness of sins solely and wholly on the basis of our Lord's completed work of atonement.

Surely, as any unbiased reader of the New Testament must see, it is as certain as can be that neither the Apostles nor the early disciples in general ever read into our Lord's words what the Roman Church has since read into them. We say again, therefore, that for the priests of Rome to claim this verse, John xx. 23, as conferring the prerogative of absolution upon *them* is as preposterous as it is perverse.

Even the Roman Catholic Church did not resort to misusing our text until more recent centuries. It was at the fourth Lateran Council, in A.D. 1215, that Pope Innocent III officially instituted auricular confession to priests as a canonical article of the Roman faith; and it is since then that John xx. 23 has increasingly acquired its new meaning! But the Roman dogma of auricular confession to priests was thrown out by the Reformers of the sixteenth century, along with other such perversions and corruptions of the Gospel. Nor can there be any doubt that the Reformers were right, if we adhere to the Scriptures, for the New Testament knows no more of *confession* to priests than of *absolution* by priests.

To bolster up such confession to priests by the supposed support of James v. 16, "Confess your faults one to another", is as childishly monstrous as it is to invest priests with the supposed power to absolve sin on the pretext of John xx. 23. The confiding of faults referred to in James v. 16 is just as obviously mutual, social, and reciprocal as it is obviously *not* sacerdotal.

Of course, the Roman Catholic misappropriation of John xx. 23 is just an incidental to the whole sacramental system by which that church has degenerated the Christian minister into a priest, the Lord's table into an altar, and the Lord's Supper into a supposedly flesh-and-blood perpetuation of the crucifixion. A "priest" must not only have a sacrifice which he can offer, but the power to grant remission. Thus the Christian believer is shut up to the response or refusal of a hierarchy with powers which unrecognisably outclass those of the first apostolate! This hierarchy administers (supposedly) a vast "Thesaurus Ecclesiae" or accumulated spiritual treasury from which spiritual benefactions are imparted to the faith. Father Thurston, a Jesuit, thus describes it: "The infinite merits of Christ our Redeemer, and the superabundant penance of the Saints, who offered to God a greater atonement than was required for the expiation of their own sins, were conceived of as creating a fund of satisfactions which the Church dispenses at will, and which she applies to those offenders who seem specially to deserve her favour."

To us Protestant and evangelical Christians such nonsense is not only comic—it is blasphemous. We regard it as a super-insult to the Calvary work of God's incarnate Son.

Alas, how brimful is the fulfilment of the New Testament forecast that worldly and fleshly corruptions would enter into and disfigure the organised church! None of the aforementioned innovations finds place in the apostolic or sub-apostolic church. In his Apology to the Roman emperor, Justin Martyr (martyred about A.D. 165) wrote: "I say also that prayers and thanksgivings are the only sacrifices which are well-pleasing to God. These alone have Christians been instructed to offer, even in the memorial of food and drink by which they commemorate the Passion which the Son of God suffered for them."

Look at the simplicity of that first church; then look at the Roman Catholic Church of today! Could anyone honestly recognise the former in the latter? Mind you, we realise only too well what an appeal the decoratively and diplomatically and theatrically elaborated Roman system makes to the flesh, to the "natural" man who wants to feel safe and good through being "very religious". The Roman Church takes the laurels for clever appeal to natural sentiment, emotion, and gullibility. D. M. Petre, himself a Roman Catholic, says truly enough, "In the Church of Rome, with her richly pagan character, the idolatrous instincts of the human heart have freer play than in the Reformed Churches."

Let us say it again, with final emphasis: In the New Testament the only confession which brings remission of sin is confession to GOD, as in 1 John i. 9: "If we confess our sins, HE is faithful and righteous to forgive us our sins, and to cleanse us from all un-righteousness." And the only true absolution from sin comes to us direct from Christ himself, through the merits of His full, free, finished and final atonement for sin—*One* for all, and *once* for all. That was the way of remission which Peter himself proclaimed on that never-to-be-forgotten Day of Pentecost long ago: "Repent and be baptised, every one of you, in the Name of Jesus Christ,

for the remission of sins; and ye shall receive the gift of the Holy
Spirit" (Acts ii. 38). Why, even the famous Cardinal Bellarmine,
that prince of papal controversialists, was only too relieved to
come right back to this when he lay dying, in 1621. On being
asked, "What is it that saves a soul?" he then replied, "*It is
safest to trust only in the merits of Christ.*"

The fact is, that like most other texts in the Bible which have
been a problem to readers, John xx. 23 would never have been
any problem at all if it had been read with due reference to its
setting. Let us not allow the misunderstandings which have
beclouded it to obscure the tremendous truth which it emphasizes.
The central, glorious news which it breaks to us is that of *THE
REMISSION OF SINS.* Lay hold of those two words, "*sins
. . . remitted.*" To all of us who have become exercised about
our sins this is surely the most amazing and glad-sounding
amnesty which ever came to condemned offenders. And who
among us can really ponder this matter of our personal sin and
guilt before God *without* becoming exercised? Those people of
the world who glibly boast that they do not worry about their
sins or about God or the eternal hereafter are not heroes; they
are the victims of consummate folly. However common it may
be, it is a form of strange insanity for responsible human beings
such as we are *not* to be gravely concerned about our sins and
their consequences in the life to come.

Who will dare claim to be without sins? Who will seriously
deny that conscience inwardly warns us of our accountability to
God? Who will honestly deny that in our truest moments we
realize only too clearly our guilt before God, and our need of
salvation? Men may profess belief in Evolution, may pretend
that sin is not really sin at all, and call it just an "incident" in
humanity's upward struggle; yet deep down in their consciousness the real convictions of their hearts contradict the hypothetical
opinions of their heads. Thank God, when the Holy Spirit tears
away Satan's veil from our inward eyes, and we become divinely
convicted of our guilt, the Gospel of Christ comes with its message
of blood-bought pardon!

I suppose that Richard the First is reckoned to be about the
bravest of the English kings. Because of his daring and prowess
in battle he became called Richard Coeur-de-Lion. But he was

also a very generous-hearted man. When his treacherous brothe
John, who had tried to rob him of his crown, pleaded for merc
Richard said: "I forgive him, and I hope to forget his injuri
as easily as he will forget my pardon." Perhaps most of us hav
heard about his remarkable forgiveness of the man who kille
him. One of his French vassals, Vidomar of Limoges, had rebelle
against him, and Richard with his army besieged him in h
castle at Châluz. At one point during the siege, with fateful di
regard of danger, the king ventured too near the castle wall
almost wholly unattended, and was mortally wounded by a
arrow from the bow of a young man named Bertrand de Gurda
While Richard lay dying in his tent the castle was taken an
the young man made prisoner. Heavily ironed, Bertrand wa
taken before the dying king. Imagine his emotion as he hear
Richard say: "Youth, I forgive you my death," and then (
the soldiers), "Let him go free, and give him a hundred shillings.
As they took the chains from his wrists and ankles would no
gratitude and admiration take the place of hate and rebellion i
his heart? The king's forgiveness and generosity were so ur
deserved by him. Here he was, with the past forgiven, the presen
freed, and even the future provided for by the benevolence o
the king himself whom he had cruelly wronged!

And such is the message of the Gospel to us, though in a
infinitely sublimer way. The very One whom our sins nailed t
Calvary's cross is the King of kings who now brings us a full an
free and final forgiveness through the merits of His substitu
tionary suffering. Perhaps it is not surprising that Richard
words concerning Bertrand de Gurdun were disregarded after th
king's death, and that the young man was put to a cruel death
Richard could not rise from the dead to see that his words wer
carried out. But the royal Saviour who died for us on Calvar
has risen, and lives with power to make the Gospel real in ou
experience.

Oh, those pierced hands which bring us such free and yet suc
dearly-purchased pardon! Oh, that riven side from which ther
flows the redeeming love of God to us unworthy sinners! Ho
great a thing must be the forgiveness of sins if it cost *that*! Truly
where sin abounds, the grace of God has much more abounded

TOTAL ABOLITION OF WAR!
—Isaiah ix. 5.

We sing a hope supreme,
  Outlasting death and time;
Its never-ending vistas gleam
  With prospects all sublime.

Our Lord shall reappear,
  And sleeping ones arise,
And we, transfigured, who remain
  Shall join them in the skies!

Our Lord's millennial reign
  On earth we then shall share;
As King of all, the Lamb once slain
  Shall bless men everywhere.

Then on, beyond all thought,
  Through ages—perfect bliss!
Oh may we count the "world" as nought
  For such a hope as this!

TOTAL ABOLITION OF WAR!

" For every battle of the warrior is with confused noise, and garments rolled in blood; but this shall be with burning and fuel of fire." Isaiah ix. 5.

LOOK carefully at this verse. It has a wonderful message, especially for our own days; yet as it reads in the Authorized Version its real meaning is regrettably obscured. It is followed by the oft-sung and oft-quoted words of Messianic prophecy: "For unto us a Child is born, unto us a Son is given; and the government shall be upon His shoulder: and His name shall be called Wonderful, Counsellor, The Mighty God, The Everlasting Father, The Prince of Peace. Of the increase of His government and peace, there shall be no end, upon the throne of David, and upon His kingdom, to order it and to establish it with justice from henceforth even for ever" (verses 6 and 7).

This seemingly obscure fifth verse, therefore, has a magnificent sequel; but reading it as it now appears in the Authorized rendering the puzzle is to decipher just what its precise connection is with the Messianic prediction which follows it. Some time ago a thoughtful reader expressed the double problem of this verse to us as follows. First, what is the point of the verse itself, seeing that its two clauses seem quite unrelated? Second, what is the relevance of the verse to the verses which follow it, seeing that it is linked to verse 6 by the conjunction, "For," and yet seems strangely foreign to it? Both these questions are answered together by readjusting the translation of it into English.

As the verse now stands it seems merely to suggest a not very vivid contrast between two sorts of battle—one with "confused noise and garments rolled in blood," and the other with "burning and fuel of fire." But that is simply due (much as we dislike to criticize our dear old Authorized Version) to a faulty translation of the Hebrew into English here. Let us therefore get the correct translation. In the second clause of the verse, which says, "but this shall be with burning and fuel of fire," the preposition *"with"* must be changed to *"for,"* as in later translations; and this one little alteration transforms the sense of the whole verse. The true rendering then is substantially this:

> *For all the armour of the armed man in the onset, and the cloak rolled in blood, shall be for burning, even food for the fire.*

The American Standard gives it: "For all the armour of the armed man in the tumult, and the garments rolled in blood, shall even be for burning, for fuel of fire." So then, this verse is really a prophecy of the time when war shall be utterly done away, when military weapons and apparel shall be fuel for the fire. And when the verse is thus read, not only does it admirably consummate the picture of prosperity given in the preceding verses, by declaring that even the implements and blood-stained clothing of warfare shall be utterly consumed, but it connects itself vitally with the famous and thrilling Messianic prophecy which crowns it. The *reason* why war shall be done away is, "*FOR* unto us a Child is born, unto us a Son is given . . . the Prince of *PEACE* . . . Of the increase of His government and of *PEACE* there shall be no end . . ." So now, as Christian believers, in a war-weary world, let us gratefully re-read this prophetic promise again, as given in truer rendering.

"FOR ALL THE ARMOUR OF THE ARMED MAN IN THE TUMULT, AND THE GARMENTS ROLLED IN BLOOD, SHALL EVEN BE FOR BURNING, FOR FUEL OF FIRE. FOR UNTO US A CHILD IS BORN; UNTO US A SON IS GIVEN; AND THE GOVERNMENT SHALL BE UPON HIS SHOULDER; AND HIS NAME SHALL BE CALLED WONDERFUL, COUNSELLOR, MIGHTY GOD, EVERLASTING FATHER, PRINCE OF PEACE. OF THE INCREASE OF HIS GOVERNMENT AND OF PEACE THERE SHALL BE NO END, UPON THE THRONE OF DAVID, AND UPON HIS KINGDOM, TO ESTABLISH IT, AND TO UPHOLD IT WITH JUDGMENT AND WITH RIGHTEOUSNESS FROM HENCEFORTH EVEN FOR EVER. THE ZEAL OF THE LORD OF HOSTS SHALL PERFORM THIS."

LITERAL OR OTHERWISE?

But this "problem" text provokes further reflection, for although we now see it in its corrected translation and in its contextual coherence, there still remains what to many minds is a measurelessly bigger problem. This text predicts *the total abolition of war*. The "armour of the armed man" and the "cloak rolled in blood" are to become "fuel for the fire." War is to be so completely and finally done away that the very weapons and implements and uniforms of war are to be scrapped and burned. What a consoling, heartening, captivating picture that would be to the present war-sickened peoples of Europe and Asia, if only they could be certain that it would come true! But then the prophet's words were written about two thousand seven hundred years ago; and from that time to this, history has been one long chain of wars, big and little, an ever-recurring plague upon the common people, and a continuous scourge of suffering, sorrow, and tears. Moreover, in recent times, the weapons of war have become so much more deadly and destructive, and the scale of operations so much more expansive, that wars are more fearful now than even our fiercest ancestors ever dreamed they could be; and Isaiah's prediction seems less likely of fulfilment than ever. Do not the two-and-a-half millenniums between Isaiah and ourselves prove that his prediction was merely wishful thinking?

Well, there is the problem; and, of course, it involves the inspiration of the Bible. Is Isaiah's prediction here to be taken literally? Or is it just a kind of prophetic hyperbolism, imaginative idealism, florid Orientalism, poetic exaggeration? If it was meant to be taken literally, then in view of the subsequent record of history from then until now, has not the promise broken down miserably? And if the promise has broken down, what about the inspiration of the Bible? Or is it credible that Isaiah's prediction is *still* to come true, despite this long, long lapse of war-cursed history?

Yes, that is the problem. What about an answer? Well, to begin with, let us settle it in our minds that this prediction was meant to be taken *literally*. How do we know that? We know it, among other reasons, because it falls into exactly the same category as scores and scores of other predictions which were meant to be taken literally, and many of which have already *been fulfilled accordingly* in subsequent history. What about all the remarkable prophecies of Isaiah and Jeremiah and Ezekiel and other prophets, concerning Tyre and Sidon and Egypt and Nineveh and Babylon and Edom and the Jews? In some of their details, some of these predictions seemed almost impossible of fulfilment when they were written, yet they were fulfilled to the letter. What about all the wonderful predictions concerning the coming Christ? Think of the many strange and striking, and sometimes seemingly contradictory features, in those scores and scores of Messianic prophecies which afterward came true in every detail, in the life of our Lord Jesus on earth. There is no greater argument for the inspiration of the Bible than this great mass of fulfilled prophecy; for however many wonderful things man can do in these days of science and discovery, there is one thing that he cannot do, and will never be able to do, and which no being in the universe can do, except God, and that is to tell the future. That is the solitary prerogative of the Creator; and, therefore, fulfilled prophecy such as we have in the Bible, is the absolutely indisputable seal of divine inspiration.

To branch off here, to discuss fulfilled prophecy, would be a digression requiring a book all to itself; but in point of fact, no such digression is needed, for many able books have now been written on Bible prophecy. And who can read, for instance, Keith's great work on Bible prophecy, or that fascinating little book, *Wonders of Prophecy*, by the late John Urquhart, without seeing, not only that hundreds of predictions have already been fulfilled with clear and exact historical correspondence, but that those other predictions, which relate to time still future, are just as clearly meant to be taken literally, and are just as certain of a true fulfilment? One of these latter is the "problem" text we are now considering, Isaiah ix. 5. A hundred Bible predictions already fulfilled in history rise up to attest that *this* prediction, concerning the abolition of war, is also to be taken literally. And many another prophecy which is *not* yet fulfilled, but which is clearly to have a concrete, historical fulfilment, supports this. Isaiah ix. 5 is not an exception to the rule. Nor is it the only prediction which envisages a warless era in futurity. It fits in quite normally as a component part of the whole scheme of Scripture prophecy, and beyond all doubt is meant to be taken literally.

Furthermore, the *context* of the prediction shows that it is to be taken literally. See what follows?—

> " *For unto us a child is born;*
> *Unto us a son is given.*"

Did *that* come true in actual fact? It did. It came true in the birth and life of our Lord Jesus; and the strict exactness of the parallel ideas in the prophecy has often been pointed out. Our Lord is both the "child" who is "born" and the "son" who is "given." As to His *human* nature, He is the "child" who is "born." As to His *divine* nature, He is the "son" who is "given." Note that the "child" is "*born*"—for the Bethlehem miracle was the *beginning* of a new life. Note that the "son" is "*given*"—for before ever He became incarnate by that mysterious miracle at Bethlehem, He was the pre-incarnate and eternal Son of God. But read on a bit further—

> "*And the government shall be upon His shoulder; and His name shall be called Wonderful, Counsellor, the Mighty God, the Everlasting Father, the Prince of Peace. Of the increase of His government there shall be no end, upon the throne of David. . . .*"

Is *that* yet to come true in actual fact? It is. How do we know? Well, if the Gospel-writer, Luke, is to be trusted (and to ourselves, of course, he *is* to be trusted), an angel came to Mary, the mother of our Lord, and *confirmed* this prophecy of Isaiah. See Luke i. 31–3—"Thou shalt bring forth a Son, and shalt call His name, JESUS. He shall be great, and shall be called the Son of the Highest; and the Lord God shall give unto Him the throne of His father David; and He shall reign over the house of Jacob for ever." By no stretch of imagination can it be said that those words of the angel, based upon the prophecy of Isaiah, have yet been fulfilled. To try to spiritualize them into referring to the *Church* and to a *spiritual* reign over the hearts of Christian believers is sheer imposition and distortion. The present age of grace and of the Church is a long and gracious suspension period in which the Davidic kingdom is historically in abeyance; but if language, both in the Old Testament and in the New, has any honest meaning at all, our Lord Jesus is to come again and occupy the Davidic throne, and to reign in world-wide Messianic empire. Yes, the *context* of Isaiah ix. 5 is to be taken literally, and so is our "problem" text itself.

THE WONDERFUL PROSPECT

So, then, our text, Isaiah ix. 5, predicts the total abolition of war; it is to be taken literally; and it will yet come true, just as certainly as hundreds of other prophecies in the pages of Holy Writ. This gives rise to certain considerations, three of which it is pertinent to mention here.

First, *the only true hope of world peace and the abolition of war is in Christ.* We emphasize that adjective, "true"—the only *true* hope of ending war is in Christ. There have been other hopes, but they have failed. There *still are* other hopes, but they also will fail. From the beginning of the twentieth century up to the time of the Great War of 1914–18, the great idea was that increasing *education* was sure eventually to abolish war; and this idea was greatly reinforced by the fact that most of the eminent scientists had espoused the theory of Evolution (as also, alas, had far too many leaders and thinkers among the churches), which seemed to imply that man was necessarily making upward progress toward ultimate utopia. But the 1914–18 war came as an ugly shock; and education was seen going "hand in glove" with the most cleverly and coldly calculated cruelty ever known in the history of wars. Then, between that war and the still greater war of 1939–45, the popular hope was the League of Nations, accompanied by a revived belief in the theory of Evolution, and a new insistence on social improvement and the sacredness of international treaties. Moreover, it was assumed that in view of the fact that the weapons of war had now become so frightful and devastating, no nation would ever again *dare* to start a new war. Quite apart from its ghastly carnage in the physical realm, the 1939–45 war came as a prostrating *mental* shock to thousands of thinking people (whose thinking had not been quite thoughtful enough!), who had placed their fond hopes on the seeming progress of civilization. The League of Nations was shown to be merely a league of *notions*; and the German culture-race let loose on Europe its hordes of educated, Nazi human-demons. There is no solid hope in education, leagues of nations, international charters, and so on. The root trouble is *the human heart itself*. Christ alone is the true hope of an enduring world-peace, and that for two reasons: first, He alone can really regenerate the human heart; second, He is soon to return to this earth to set up a world-wide empire which will absolutely exclude war.

There are two noticeable features about present-day thought concerning war. First, there is everywhere a sense of the desperate urgency that something *must* be done to eliminate war, in view of the extreme pitch of destructiveness now reached by the *weapons* of war. Second, there is nothing like such sanguine hope to-day as there was between the last two wars, that war *will* be abolished by anything that human leaders can do. Sadly one hears and reads wonderings and fearings about "the next war." By the time Christ returns, the point will actually have been reached where the peoples of the earth *despair* of permanent peace apart from divine intervention. It will by then be *realized* that Christ is the only hope, and that apart from Him, humanity would destroy itself.

But we must add a further observation. The wonderful prospect of the abolition of war, which our text sets before us, is connected with *a visible return and reign of the Lord Jesus*. He will stand again on the Mount of Olives. He will come again, as Israel's King. He will take the throne of David, and will reign in Jerusalem. The Lamb of God shall rule as the Lion of Judah. There may be differences of opinion regarding different aspects of Christ's second coming, as it is taught to us in the Scriptures, but as to the *fact* that His yet-future return is taught in the Scriptures, there can surely be no genuine doubt. We do not wish to sound intolerant, but quite frankly we are completely unable to understand those people who say they cannot see a visible return of Christ foretold in the New Testament. As clearly as language can possibly express it, that hope is set before us.

Nothing in all Scripture is more repeatedly and explicitly predicted. It has been figured out that on the average our Lord's
second coming is referred to, in the New Testament, once in
every twenty-seven verses! They are surely queer eyes which
can see, in verses like Acts i. 11 and 1 Thessalonians iv. 16, 17,
and Revelation i. 7, not to mention a score of others, anything
but a personal, visible, glorious, and yet-future return of Christ.

With the Bible open before us, we ourselves believe and teach
that there will be no final abolition of war until this visible
return and reign of the Lord Jesus Christ takes place. Does
this mean that we will not do anything, or take part in any
movement, to avert war meanwhile? No; it does not mean that
at all. Our Lord told us that the poor we should always have
with us; but does that withhold us from constant effort to relieve
poverty? The Scriptures make clear that at the time of our
Lord's return there will be millions who ignore or reject the
Gospel, but does that give us reason to slack off from daily endea-
vour to lead souls to Christ? Quite plainly we learn from the
words of our Lord and His Apostles that the Millennium is not
to be brought in by the gradual spreading abroad of the Christian
ethic, or even by the evangelization of all the earth's peoples;
yet we find no reason there for flagging in our efforts to let
"every creature" know the wonderful news of salvation through
the Cross of Calvary.

No; our Scripturally-founded conviction, that there will be no
abolition of war apart from the visible return and reign of Christ,
does not make us unsympathetically sceptical or coldly unco-
operative; but it does help us the more wisely to direct our
efforts and to put our emphases in the right places. Deep down
in our hearts we know that there can be no enduring world-peace
apart from our Lord's return; and, as we preach the Gospel,
we keep on stressing this fact to leaders and people, and thus seek
to hasten the day of His coming. There are Scriptural indications
that we *can* hasten that day. 2 Peter iii. 12, when rightly translated, reads: "*Looking for and hastening the day of God.*" While
God does not leave His larger purposes for the human race at
the mercy of the uncertain will of man, He does nevertheless
leave enough scope for the genuine free scope of the human will
to ensure that at all times men know that they are acting and

deciding according to their own choice. It thus comes about that there is a certain *contingency* adhering to the second coming of Christ. It is contingent, as Romans xi. 25 indicates, upon the gathering in of the "fulness of the Gentiles"; and it would seem, therefore, that we are definitely "hastening the day" of our Lord's return as we seek to gather in precious souls to Christ. "Even so, Lord Jesus, come quickly!"

Oh, what a prospect this is, which our text sets before us! Think of it again—war abolished, the implements of war turned into "fuel for the fire," a millennium of unbroken peace! What arresting pictures Isaiah gives us of that time!—

"And He (Christ) shall judge among the nations, and shall rebuke many people; and they shall beat their swords into plowshares, and their spears into pruning hooks: nation shall not lift up sword against nation, neither shall they learn war any more."

"With righteousness shall He judge the poor, and reprove with equity for the meek of the earth: and He shall smite the earth with the rod of his mouth, and with the breath of His lips shall he slay the wicked. And righteousness shall be the girdle of His loins, and faithfulness the girdle of His reins. The wolf also shall dwell with the lamb, and the leopard shall lie down with the kid, and the calf and the young lion and the fatling together; and a little child shall lead them. And the cow and the bear shall feed; their young ones shall lie down together; and the lion shall eat straw like the ox . . . They shall not hurt nor destroy in all my holy mountain; for the earth shall be full of the knowledge of Jehovah, as the waters cover the sea!"—Isaiah ii. 4; xi. 4–9.

Will it really come to pass? Well, turn to our text again—

"For all the armour of the armed man in the onset, and the cloak rolled in blood, shall be for burning, even fuel for the fire."

Now look at the verse after it—

"For unto us a Child is born, unto us a Son is given; and the government shall be upon His shoulder . . . the Prince of Peace."

And now see the divine guarantee at the end of the next verse again—

"THE ZEAL OF THE LORD OF HOSTS WILL PERFORM THIS."

Yes, it will really happen—and perhaps sooner than most of us are daring to think; because *GOD* has said it, and He never breaks His word!

This is a day when many hearts are downcast. It is only too easy to look down just now. Anxiety spreads abroad. There is disturbance everywhere. Apostasy cripples Christendom. Godlessness abounds. Every age has had its own besetting evils; but, when full allowance has been made for all similarities between the present and the past, the present world-situation is plainly without precedent. When statesmen of former generations foreboded wars, what were the wars which *they* feared compared with the civilization-destroying potentialities of modern warfare? When in all history were things on such a race-embracing scale as to-day? When were there such earth-girdling and highly organized anti-God movements? When were there such portentous scientific discoveries? The widespread concern at the present situation is no empty scare.

The one real hope is the return of Christ. The very phenomena which, in themselves, might well make our hearts fail for fear are the *signs* that He is soon to come. The darker grows the night, the nearer draws the dawn!

> What of the night, O watchman?
> Turn to the East thine eyes;
> And say is there any token
> Of the dawning in the skies?
> Or do the shadows linger,
> Thy lips, are they sad and dumb
> With never a word of gladness
> That the tarrying morn is come?
>
> Then answered the patient watchman
> From the mountain's lonely height,
> To the waiting souls in the valley,
> I can see the breaking light!

There's a glow on the far horizon
  That is growing more wide and clear;
And soon shall the sun be flinging
  His splendours both far and near!

What of the night, O Watchman?
  Rises to Thee our cry.
Prophet divine of Nazareth,
  Make to our hearts reply.
Over the earth's wild warfare
  Comes not a time more fair?
Swords into ploughshares beaten?
  Peace reigning everywhere?

Wait, saith the heavenly Watchman;
  Let not the spirit quail;
Strife shall not be eternal;
  Harmony shall prevail.
Battle-clouds all shall scatter;
  Hatred shall be outcast;
Love's ever-broadening glory
  Break o'er the world at last!

DOES JESUS DRAW "ALL MEN"?

—John xii. 32.

DOES JESUS DRAW "ALL MEN"?

*"And I, if I be lifted up from the earth, will draw all men
unto Me."* John xii. 32.

ONE OF the most remarkable characteristics of Christ's preaching
was its sublime egoism. He did not merely declare truth; He
said, "I am the truth." He did not merely proclaim a Gospel;
He Himself is the Gospel. Nowhere is this egoism more arresting
than in our text. Jesus here prophesies that He will draw all
men to Himself. It seems a staggering prediction to have risked;
yet there it is, uttered with measured deliberateness.

There are two notable features belonging to this prediction,
which at once arrest attention; first, the seeming unlikeliness of
its fulfilment, at the time when it was uttered; second, the
remarkable actuality of its fulfilment in subsequent history. In
connection with the second of these two features, a problem
arises which it is well for us to face and try to settle. Let us
briefly consider first, the seeming unlikeliness of fulfilment at the
time when this prediction was uttered.

SEEMING UNLIKELINESS OF FULFILMENT

Few prophecies could ever have seemed less likely to come
true than did this one, judging by the outward circumstances at
the time of its utterance.

Consider the *person* who utters this prediction concerning
himself. Who is He that dares to entertain such a vast prospect?
Must He be taken seriously? The claim assumes the racial
centrality and supremacy of the speaker! On any merely human
lips the words would be consummate conceit and preposterous
pride. How often have ambitious dreamers dreamed of world
domination, only to wake, sooner or later, and find their dreams
vapourizing away! Monarchs have greedily envisaged world
empire. Militarists have thought to subjugate all peoples beneath
the sword of universal conquest. Philosophers have been quite

sure that their ideas would dominate the minds of all men. Founders and promulgators of religions have been going to convert all the world to their systems. But such illusions have been dispelled again and again by the relentless ironies of experience. Such dreamers and self-confident enthusiasts have been like poultry-men counting their chickens before they were hatched, like businessmen reckoning their profits before their clients had paid up; like farmers imaginatively gathering in their harvest before it had grown in the fields, and forgetting to allow for the blight of drought and the blast of storm. Such big ideas of world-dominion or of racial magnetism have been merely colourful bubbles; castles in the air, dissolved at a breath; fools' paradises, doomed to fall about the ears of those who lived in them. We have learned to greet all such claims to world conquest, either in the physical or in the mental realm, with dubiety.

What, then, of the confident prediction in our text? Who was the speaker? Was He a king or an emperor? Was He some military commander? Was He some outstanding philosopher? No; He was none of these things, not, at least, in the usual sense of those words. He was a pilgrim preacher, without any influential earthly connections whatever. He was a plain man who "went about doing good." He was of all characters the purest, and He had wonderful gifts of healing, and He must have been a grippingly impressive preacher, despite the opposition which He aroused; yet, all the same, He was but a poor and socially obscure man.

Consider the *place* where this world-embracing prophecy of our text was uttered. If it had been spoken in the world's metropolis, with the speaker conscious of government support, and millions backing Him, willing to spill their blood to vindicate His claim, it might have been not a little impressive. But the fact is that this prediction was uttered merely to a fickle, feverish-minded gathering of folk, swollen into a curious crowd, by a wayside near the city of a vanquished nation, a nation without army or navy, and with scarcely any mentionable political status. What though this prophet of Galilee had prevailed upon His fellow-countrymen throughout the whole of His little native land? What though the whole nation had risen up under His lead, to throw off the yoke of the captor? Would it not have been as a mere "storm in a tea-cup" to the mighty powers of the Roman empire? But the fact was that even the leaders of His own people were nearly all against Him. To Pharisees, Sadducees, and Herodians alike, He was anathema. That such a one in such a place should make such a claim as this, that He would yet draw all men unto Himself, did it not seem ironic, even ludicrous?

Consider, also, the *occasion* when the great prophecy of our text was spoken. Not only was it spoken by a comparatively obscure person and in a comparatively obscure place, but it was spoken in a set of circumstances which seemed utterly unpropitious. It would be difficult to think of any occasion on which this prediction could have been uttered which would have made its fulfilment seem less likely. The brief, three-year public ministry of Jesus had passed its meridian. Opposition, dark, fierce, sinister, had more and more gathered force against Him. The kingdom of heaven, which He had proclaimed "at hand," had been rejected, first morally, then civically, officially, nationally. He had offered Himself to His people as their promised Messiah-King; but by now the repudiation of that offer was obvious. It was only a matter of days now before Jesus of Nazareth would be hanging between crucified robbers, on a felon's cross; and Jesus himself knew it. To all outward appearances it seemed as though the mission of Jesus had come to utter failure. Never did any prophecy seem less likely to be fulfilled than did this prophecy of Jesus at the time when it was uttered—"And I, if I be lifted up from the earth, will draw all men unto Me."

THE REMARKABLE FULFILMENT

But now reflect again on the wonderful way in which this prophecy has been fulfilled in subsequent history. The pretentious dreams of others have vanished in unreality; but the prediction made by Jesus concerning Himself has been, and still is being, ever-growingly fulfilled. Two eventful millenniums have increasingly demonstrated His sublime solitariness, His historical supremacy, and His universal appeal to men. Millions have been savingly drawn to Him in every generation. He has altered the whole course of history. Nearly all the world's calendars and chronological reckonings are arranged in relation to Him. The greatest nations of the world owe their civilization to Him. The early preachers of the Gospel had not been preaching the message of the crucified and glorified Jesus for more than a few years before there was a hue and cry, "These men that have turned the world upside down are come hither also!" And to-day there are millions and millions of Christians scattered through all five continents.

Yes, there are millions, all round the globe, who name the name of Jesus with joy and faith and hope and love. The appeal of Christianity penetrates everywhere. This is not true of any other religion, nor ever can be. Mohammedanism, Buddhism, Confucianism, each of these makes its appeal in a limited geographical area. None of these could ever thrive, for instance, among us modern westerners. Yet despite opposition and misrepresentation, the appeal of Jesus more and more wins gently through, in practically all parts of the earth. What is more, there is no doubt about the fact that in these days the other great religions are tottering on their foundations. They cannot bear critical investigation as Christianity can. They begin to creak and groan and crack and break under the pressure of modern exigencies. This may not be at once apparent to the casual observer; but those who have closer knowledge know how the increasing enlightenment of the long-deluded masses is causing them to see the falsity of much in these systems by which they have been deceived. While there are many millions of people on earth to-day whose eyes have never been opened to see in the Lord Jesus Christ the one and only Saviour of the soul, it is true to say that the minds of thinking people all over the world to-day are being more and more turned toward Him as the supreme expression of moral beauty and of divine love.

But at this point we encounter *a problem*. It is a problem which has been voiced by several in our own hearing. Despite this unique and widespread appeal of Jesus, which we are only too glad to acknowledge, *has His prediction really come true to the full extent indicated in His words?* He said, "And I, if I be lifted up from the earth, will draw *all* men unto me." What about that word, "*all*"? If we are strictly honest, and strictly true to the text, are we not obliged to admit that the prediction has *not* really been fulfilled? Jesus said He would draw *all* men to

Himself; but has He done so? Apparently not. Does He draw all men to Himself even in our own country and in our own time? Apparently not. What about the many who reject Him? What about the multitudes who are neither one thing nor the other toward Him? What about the millions of the still unevangelized heathen, who have never even heard the name of Jesus? What shall we say about all these? What about that "all" in the text? Must our Lord's use of that word "all" be taken at its face value? Or is it to be understood in some modified way?

Well, this is another case where careful reference to the context provides the clear solution to the problem. To appreciate the setting of our text we must go back and begin to read at verse 20.

"There were certain Greeks among them that came up to worship at the feast. The same came to Philip, which was of Bethsaida of Galilee, and desired him, saying, Sir, we would see Jesus, Philip cometh and telleth Andrew; and again Andrew and Philip tell Jesus."

What answer, then, did our Lord send to those enquiring Greeks? Strangely enough, as it seems at first, He sent no answer at all: yet there *is* an answer implicit in the profound words which He now addressed to Andrew and Philip, and to the crowd gathered round.

"The hour is come that the Son of Man should be glorified. Verily, verily, I say unto you, Except a corn of wheat fall into the ground and die, it abideth alone; but if it die, it bringeth forth much fruit."

But what relevance had these words about the "corn of wheat" to those enquiring Greeks? The circumstances explain. Our Lord had come to the last week of His earthly life. He knew that He was rejected. The Cross was already casting its shadow upon Him. There must have been a deep sorrow and sadness in His heart at this time. He had wept over the impenitent city; but He knew that His tears were in vain. Already the leaders were plotting His death. The enquiry of those "Greeks" was a sudden, gleaming reminder that beyond the confines of little Judæa, there was a whole world stretching out yearning hands

D

for a *Saviour*. Yet while Jesus was there in Judæa and Jerusalem, offering Himself *exclusively* to the Jews, as their Messiah-King, He had no message for those Greeks and the rest of the great outside world. The "corn of wheat" must die before there could be the world-wide harvest. The Gospel of the Kingdom must give place to that larger message, the Gospel of "the grace of God which bringeth salvation to all men." The Messiah of the Jews must be crucified if He was to become the Saviour of the world. His crucifixion as the rejected King would be His coronation as *the world's Saviour*! Then, and not till then, would He have a message for those enquiring Greeks and the great world of which they were representative.

Now it is precisely here that we find the explanation of the "all" in our Lord's prediction, "I, if I be lifted up from the earth, will draw all men unto me." He does not mean all men *without exception*, but all men *without distinction*, whether Jews, or Greeks, or Romans, or of any other nationality. The uplifted Christ of Calvary is no longer simply the prophet of Galilee, offering Himself exclusively to the Jews as their Messiah; He is the Saviour of the world. Calvary obliterates all national distinctions. The Gospel is to men of all nations; and although Jesus has not drawn all men to Himself *without exception* (for the many have always rejected), yet He draws all men *WITH-OUT DISTINCTION*. In this He is unique and supreme. It was this which He clearly intended to convey when He used the word "all" in His remarkable prediction; and the prediction has come true to the full.

THE FACT AND THE REASON

How true it is, that Jesus draws all men to Himself without distinction! He draws all men, without *social* distinction—not only the Newtons and Gladstones and Ruskins, but the John Bunyans and Jerry McAuleys and Sam Hadleys as well; not only the rich and the high and the cultured, but the poor and the low and the sunken; not only the élite of society, but the "broken earthenware" of slumdom.

And Jesus draws all men to Himself, without *racial* distinction. There is not a race of people on the earth, wherever the Gospel has been preached, from which Jesus has not drawn men and women to Himself. All over the world, among whites and blacks and browns and yellows, you can find grateful human beings who rejoice to say, "Jesus is mine!" You do not find people in all parts of the world exclaiming with glad gratitude, "Mohammed is mine!" or "Buddha is mine!" Jesus has no competitor. His pull and spell over human hearts is quite alone in the way it overrides all distinctions of race and colour.

And He draws all types of people to Himself, without *age* distinction. There is that in Him which appeals to wondering, questioning, simple-hearted childhood. There is that which attracts and captivates rosy youth, and eager, questing, energetic young manhood and womanhood. Nor is the appeal of Jesus less to maturity than to youth. He arrests and holds the middle-aged. He means as much to parenthood as to childhood. His gentle constraint prevails over fathers and mothers just as over sons and daughters. And old age, as well, falls equal prey to His spell, when all other charms and engrossments of life have spent their force; for there irradiates from the face of Jesus that which gilds life's eventide with heavenly shinings. Such is the innate need and native response of the human heart in general, that at all periods of life there is an inherent susceptibility to the spiritual magnetism of Jesus. Childhood is not afraid of Him, as it lisps its "Gentle Jesus, meek and mild." Youth cannot but acclaim Him the greatest of all heroes, of whom Isaac Watts wrote—to quote his original wording,—

" When I survey the wondrous Cross,
Where *the young Prince of Glory died. . . .*"

Middle-age needs Him who was "tempted in all points like as we are," who is "touched with the feeling of our infirmities," and can "succour them that are tempted." And old age needs Him more than ever, who is strength to the weak, and the light of heaven to those whose earthly eyes are growing dim.

And *why* is it that Jesus thus draws all men to Himself, without distinction? Fundamentally, it is because all men and women have *the same spiritual need*, without distinction. We all need the love of God; and we find it in Christ, breaking forth like a glorious

river, spreading throughout the world, and submerging all the
barriers which separate men from each other. We all need a
heavenly Father's forgiveness, for we are sinners; and we find
it in Christ, provided at infinite cost. We all need inward cleansing
and regeneration; and we find both in Christ; for "the blood of
Jesus Christ, God's Son, cleanseth from all sin"; and all who
become savingly united to Him by faith are "born anew" of the
Holy Spirit. We all need hope for the future, especially for that
vast destiny beyond the grave; and in Christ we find it; for the
Sin-bearer of Calvary is the predestined King who is to bring in
the cloudless morning of a new age when sickness and sorrow and
sin and death shall be done away! In the unique and supreme
sense, Jesus Christ is the revealer of God and the redeemer of
men. In Him, and in Him alone is there *salvation from sin*;
and wherever men are conscious of sin and spiritual need, there
the drawing-power of Jesus prevails.

ARTIFICIAL "EXPLANATIONS"

So, then, when our Lord said that He would draw all men to
Himself, He did not mean all men without exception, but all
men *without distinction*. To see the import of the text thus clearly
in the light of its context saves us from any need to trot out
artificial "explanations." We have come across several of these
in relation to this "all" in our Lord's prediction.

The commonest "explanation" is that Jesus draws all men
to Himself inasmuch as He draws them either in grace or in
judgment. Those whom He does not draw in *grace*, in this present
life, He will draw to Himself in *judgment*, in the life beyond, when
He sits on the "great white throne" at the final judgment of
mankind. But surely our Lord had no such meaning in mind,
for He said that His drawing-power was to be the result of His
being "lifted up" on the Cross. We know that when our Lord
used the expression, "lifted up from the earth," He was referring
to the Cross, for John tells us so in the verse following our text.
And besides this, our Lord will not "*draw*" men to that final
judgment at the "great white throne." All will be *compelled*
whether they will or not.

It is said, also, that when our Lord spoke about drawing all men to Himself, He looked beyond the present age, and thought of the yet-future *millennial age*, when He shall reign as king over all the earth. We ourselves also look for that golden era when all men on earth shall be the devoted and adoring subjects of His gracious, glorious majesty. That crowning age of history will certainly consummate our Lord's prediction in John xii. 32; but it certainly is not that which our Saviour has in mind when He says, "And I, if I be lifted up from the earth, will draw all men unto Me." He is clearly thinking here about a drawing of men to Himself which would be immediately consequent upon His redeeming death.

That characteristic Roman Catholic notion which would make our Lord's words mean the drawing of all men *to the empire of the pope*, we may dismiss with a grim smile!

As we have shown, there is no need for any such "explanations" as these in relation to John xii. 32, if we simply allow the context to guide us as to our Lord's meaning.

IMPLICATIONS AND APPLICATIONS

We ought not to leave this text without just a final pause to appreciate certain rather obvious but greatly important implications in it.

First, let us be quick to perceive in it the unmistakable implication of *our Lord's deity*. His prediction that He would draw all men to Himself was not just the brave hope of a martyr; nor merely the buoyant optimism of a hero, able to smile in the face of Jewish religious hatred; nor simply the persevering belief of a good man that he would be more appreciated after his death than in his life. Our Lord's words were no mere guess at the future. There is the certainty and finality of divine foreknowledge in His prediction. It is the word of the Son of God, who knows the end from the beginning.

Here, also, let us observe the indication of *a divine plan*. Our Lord has just intimated that the Cross is a necessity. Except the "corn of wheat" fall into the ground and die, there cannot be the harvest. He must go to Calvary, and there be "lifted up"; yet therefrom He would fulfil the larger purpose of God, and achieve ultimate conquest over sin and Satan. That Cross, which would appear to be an unmitigated catastrophe to His followers which would seem to contradict God's righteous government, and which would be the foulest deed of human hatred, was the centre-point in the divine plan of redemption; and our Lord knew it. He knew the outcome of the Cross; and with the full plan clearly before His eyes He prophesied that He would draw all men to Himself.

And again, let us duly note the emphasis which the wording of the prediction puts on Jesus Himself: "And *I*, if *I* be lifted up from the earth, will draw all men unto *Me*." The emphasis is even stronger in the Greek. Our Lord says He will draw men to *Himself*. Nowhere in the New Testament are we promised full churches; but this is certainly true, that the way to have full churches is to have churches full of Christ. He is the great magnet. The Church in itself has no drawing power; and it is well to emphasize this just now; for our various ecclesiastical bodies are laying great emphasis on the Church as an institution. They speak about the Church this, and the Church that, and the Church the other; they tell men and women, from the pulpit and over the radio and in various pamphlets, that they need the Church. We ourselves know of no New Testament warrant for this emphasis on the Church, in Christian propaganda. The true Church of Christ never came into existence to bear witness to itself. The central reason why the majority of people pass by the Church in these days is that the Church is preaching itself instead of Christ. That is a general statement, and we are glad to acknowledge that there are many local exceptions; but the general statement, as such, is true enough. Our business is not to uplift the Church before men, but to uplift Jesus—"Jesus only"! When Jesus draws men and women to Himself they need no drawing to the Church: they come of themselves to the place where they can learn of Him and hold fellowship with His own people.

Finally, we observe that since Jesus said He would draw "all" men to Himself, *we cannot go to the wrong person with the Gospel*. All human hearts need Him. All may be saved by Him. All ought to be sought for Him. A few years ago, a friend of mine was visiting in an infirmary ward. He came to a bed where a Roman Catholic woman was lying. "You've come to the wrong person," she said; "I'm waiting for that priest who has just come into the ward." "Oh, no," said my friend, "I have not come to the wrong person; I was definitely sent to *you*." The woman looked puzzled; so he took out his New Testament and read Mark xvi. 16, "Go ye into all the world and preach the Gospel *to every creature*." "Why, my dear woman," he said, "it is impossible to go to the wrong person with the Gospel of Christ!" So it is. May we all be faithful in uplifting Him to others!

"UNTO THIS DAY"

—2 Chronicles v. 9

"UNTO THIS DAY"

"And there (in the temple) it is (i.e., the Ark) unto this day."—2 Chronicles v. 9.

IN THIS verse from the Chronicles there is a "problem" which must have provoked questioning in many a thoughtful reader's mind. It lies in that adverbial phrase, *"unto this day."* The two books of the Chronicles, like Ezra and Nehemiah, were written *after* the exile of the Jewish people in Babylonia, and after the Jewish "Remnant" (about 60,000 in all) had *returned* to Jerusalem and Judæa under the leadership of Zerubabbel (536 B.C.) and under the leadership of Ezra (458 B.C.). In fact there is reason to think that originally 1 and 2 Chronicles, Ezra, and Nehemiah formed one undivided work—one continuous set of "chronicles"; and there is nothing more likely than that Ezra himself was the author-compiler of at least the bulk of the work. This means that the *date* of compilation must fall between about 450 to 400 B.C. How then could it be said in Ezra's day (as our text says) that the "Ark" was still there, in the temple, even *"unto this day"*?—for that temple of Solomon had been burnt to the ground about one hundred and fifty years earlier, when the Babylonians sacked Jerusalem (587 B.C.).

This problem of the words "unto this day," equally applies, of course, to those several other places where the expression occurs in the Chronicles (see, for instance, 1 Chron. iv. 43; 2 Chron. viii. 8). What shall we say about it? Well, the fact is that there is no *real* problem here at all, but the *explanation* opens up a matter of great interest which it is well worth while to consider.

It is fairly plain to see, even in our English translation of the Chronicles, that 1 and 2 Chronicles are a *compilation*—a compilation from earlier documents, and this is plainer still in the original Hebrew. About fourteen of these earlier documents are actually named. These are they—

1. Book of the Kings of Israel and Judah (2 xxvii. 7).
2. A Midrash (commentary) on the above (2 xxiv. 27).
3. Words, or History, of Samuel the Seer (1 xxix. 29).
4. Words, or History, of Gad the Seer (1 xxix. 29).
5. Words, or History, of Nathan the Prophet (2 ix. 29).
6. The Prophecy of Ahijah the Shilonite (2 ix. 29).
7. The Visions of Iddo the Seer (2 ix. 29).
8. Words, or History, of Shemaiah the Prophet (2 xii. 15).
9. Work of Iddo the Prophet on Genealogies (2 xii. 15).
10. Midrash (commentary) of Iddo the Prophet (2 xiii. 22).
11. Words, or History, of Jehu, son of Hannani (2 xx. 34).
12. Acts of Uzziah, by Isaiah the Prophet (2 xxvi. 22).
13. The Vision of Isaiah the Prophet (2 xxxii. 22).
14. Words, or History, of Hozai (or the Seers) (2 xxxiii. 19).

Now it seems quite clear that some of these earlier documents
are *quoted literally*; and one evidence of this is the occurrence of
the words *"unto this day"* in several places. If Ezra (supposing
him to be the author-compiler) had been using only the *substance*
of what some of these earlier writings contained, he would never
have used the words, "unto this day"; but (probably as an
indication of the exactness and genuineness of his use of these
earlier authorities) he incorporated their *literal wording*, yes, even
such words as "unto this day"—knowing, of course, that his
Jewish readers would well enough understand the words "unto
this day," to refer to the time of the earlier writer whom he,
Ezra, was quoting. It is well that modern readers should bear
this in mind.

But now, think a little further about these earlier documents,
these sources of compilation. They are more important and
revealing than might seem at a passing glance. They indicate
the following four very important facts:

1. That the author-compiler of the Chronicles was well-
   informed, and well-qualified on that score for the task which
   he had undertaken;
2. That he was using well-known and fully accredited documents as his authorities, which proved the *bona-fide* nature
   of his work.

3. That many consultable records and other writings, by competent and godly scholars, had accumulated during the nation's history, which fact confirms to ourselves the reliability of the records that have now come down to us in our Bible;

4. That Israel's archives were by no means the spurious, spasmodic, almost fungus growth that some of our modern "scholars" have supposed, but a carefully composed, collected, compared, and compiled body of literature.

Now even if these things were *not* so, we would still believe (on other quite adequate grounds) in the divine inspiration and inerrancy of the holy Scriptures as originally given; yet these points from the Chronicler's use of such earlier documents have real value as a confirmatory witness to the reliability of Old Testament records, and they will appeal to the more reasoning type of mind. These penmen of Scripture, so often said by a certain class of recent "scholars" to have been wonderfully careless about facts and figures and dates, could have taught the German schools of the "higher criticism" a good deal in the way of *real* carefulness. However, the historians of the Old Testament are coming into their own again at last. Perhaps no part of the Old Testament has been more confidently assailed by our modern critics than Second Kings and the two books of the Chronicles; and this part of the Old Testament has now been vindicated by the discoveries and decipherings of our archæologists more than any other.

Incidentally, some of these earlier works quoted by the Chronicler are highly interesting. We wish we had time to comment on them all. However, take the one which heads our list—"The Book of the Kings of Israel and Judah." Three times we find this title (2 Chron. xxvii. 7, xxxv. 27, xxxvi. 8). Four times we find the title partly reversed to "The Book of the Kings of Judah and Israel" (2 Chron. xvi. 11, xxv. 26, xxviii. 26, xxxii. 32). The two titles refer to the same work, as is clear from the fact that whichever way the title occurs, the reference is to a king of *Judah*. It may quite probably be that two different works on the two lines of kings had been unified into one by the time of our Chronicler.

At any rate, this "Book of the Kings" on which our Chronicler drew was a most interesting and informing collection of material.

It seems to have been nothing less than a full repertory of historical and biographical data—of the "acts" and the "wars" and the "ways" of the different kings (2 Chron. xxvii. 7). It seems a great pity that it perished—and the making of that remark leads to a further remark, namely, it is well to realize that when the Chronicler refers to this earlier work, "The Book of the Kings of Israel and Judah," he is not meaning the earlier books in our Bible, which *we* now call the Books of the Kings. On the contrary, there is good reason to think that both Kings and Chronicles in our Bible quote this same *earlier* work which the Chronicler quoted. This is indicated by the fact that the books which *we* now call 1 and 2 Kings do not contain those matters which the Chronicler says are in the book which *he* then knew as the Book of the Kings.

Perhaps to some readers these matters are of no enrapturing interest; but those who most love our precious Bible are glad to glean in any fields which yield confirmation and information concerning it. All kinds of substantiations and enlightening connections lie just between the lines, and we should keep a keen eye for them as we read or study the Scriptures from time to time.

Next time we come across that little phrase, "unto this day," in our reading of the Scriptures, let us just pause and be grateful that instead of having hit against a problem, we have come upon one more incidental indication of the reliability of the Scripture records.

THE TEMPLE, THE ARK, AND TO-DAY

We may make an up-to-date application of our text. Glance at it again: "And there (in the temple) it is (i.e., the ark) unto this day." It speaks to us of the temple and the ark; and that, in turn, speaks to us of the *unifying idea running through the two books of the Chronicles*. It is well that we should appreciate this unifying idea which runs through the Chronicles because it has a solemn and pertinent message for us to-day.

Now most people have the idea that the books of the Chronicles are just a repetition, with casual variations, of what we have in Samuel and Kings. That idea is quite erroneous. They are not merely a repetition; they are a *reconsideration* with a view to emphasizing a vital lesson. Read these two books of the Chronicles side by side with Samuel and Kings, and what do you find? Why, the variations are not casual at all. Many matters found in Samuel and Kings are *excluded* here, and many other matters which are absent from Samuel and Kings are *included* here; and it does not require a very concentrated observation to see that the omissions and additions all conform to one unifying emphasis and purpose. All the way through 1 and 2 Chronicles the emphasis is upon the *TEMPLE*. We wish we could go more fully into this, but our present limits forbid it. However, it certainly is so, the emphasis all through is on the temple.

And *why* does this retrospective collection of Chronicles put all the emphasis on the temple? The answer is found in the date of their compilation. They were compiled *after the Babylonian exile*, when the Jewish "Remnant" had returned from Babylonia to Judæa, under Zerubbabel and Ezra. This is made absolutely certain by statements and references in the Chronicles themselves. They were specially written for those repatriated Jews and their descendants who were to reconstitute Jewish national life in the homeland. If we imagine ourselves back in Judæa with those returned Jews, we soon realize that there is one very great lack which forces itself upon the mind, namely, there is no king; *THE DAVIDIC THRONE IS GONE!*

What that meant to thoughtful Jews requires little imagination to appreciate. The throne of David was unique in the earth. It was founded on a divine covenant. Yet now it was no longer there. This must have been a sore problem to thoughtful Jews. But what we stress here is that the people were returning, not now to rebuild a throne, but a *temple*. The temple was now, above all things, the symbol of the unity of the nation, and the reminder of the nation's high calling, and the sign that Jehovah was still among His chosen people, and the focus-point of that which was truest in the national life. It was in the light of that temple that all the past was to be read, and the present reconstructed, and the future anticipated. Hence the compiling of the Chronicles with their sustained emphasis on the temple and the religious aspect of things. And hence the central *purpose* of the Chronicles, namely, to bring home afresh to the covenant people where the true emphasis in Israel's national life lay, to convince them where their first duty and their only true safety lay, and thereby to challenge the elect race to a renewed consecration as the divinely appointed priest of the nations.

Let us note well that before ever Nehemiah was sent of God to rebuild the *city*, Zerubbabel and Ezra were sent to rebuild the *temple*. In any national reconstruction we must begin there. Apply this to our post-war world. Our political reconstructors will not learn the lesson, the repeated lesson of history. They persist in the worldly-wise idea that the *city* must be built before the temple. Well, they are wrong; and war will destroy their city again before it is properly built. We must begin with the *temple*! In other words, we must begin with *GOD*—or we shall fail every time.

A final word: our "problem" text tells us that the *ark* of the covenant was given the place of honour in that old-time temple of Solomon. Read that fifth chapter of 2 Chronicles again. With what reverence and dignity and honour that sacred ark was brought into the holy temple! And what a divine response there was to this honouring of the ark!—a cloud of glory filled the temple, so that "the priests could not stand to minister by reason of the cloud, for the glory of Jehovah had filled the house of God" (verse 14).

We would say to the Christian ministers of our land: Is it not time we restored the ark to its rightful place in the temple? Is it not time we gave the Bible the honoured place and the supreme regard which our fathers gave to it? Would our Protestant sanctuaries have sunk to their present numerical paucity and spiritual poverty if the rude, irreverent hand of Modernist pseudo-scholarship had not cast reproach upon the inspired oracles? The veracity and validity and vitality of Protestant Christianity are bound up with the Bible. It was because the Reformers broke through Romanist tradition and superstition, and went right to the Bible, that the glorious Reformation set us free. We are the people of that book. It is the ark of the covenant to us—of the new covenant in Christ's blood. It claims to be the inspired word of God. Through generations it has proved itself to be so. But to-day it is dishonoured, ironically enough, in the name of "Biblical scholarship"! Thousands of ministers are carrying on spiritually powerless ministries because of their broken-down attitude toward the Bible. To *their* minds it contains folk-lore, myth, error, in no small amount. Those of us who believe (some of us after much study) in the *plenary* inspiration and divine authority of the Bible are looked upon as strangely out-of-date. Yet the findings of our archæologists are more and more confirming the older view of the Bible; and also, in those places where the pure, full, glorious Gospel of the New Testament is preached, the Holy Spirit sets His seal as He does nowhere else, in the conversion of souls to Christ.

The main reason why modern Protestantism is so weakened is its defective attitude to the Bible. If we are shaky there we are shaky everywhere. The biggest division between Christians is no longer that between one denomination and another, but that (which now exists inside each denomination) between those who accept the Bible as the plenarily inspired word of God and those who do not. There is more fellowship between an Episcopalian and a Baptist who both accept the plenary inspiration of the Scriptures than there is between two co-denominationalists who do not. We may hold conferences galore about the grave break-away from the churches, but there will never be unity of purpose and action until there is unity of conviction about the Bible.

This is not to limit the right of every man to interpret for himself what is *in* the Bible. There has never been complete uniformity of *interpretation*—hence our diversity of denomination; but there *must* be unity of *attitude toward* the Bible, or there is simply no final authority, and *all* our Protestant bodies are thrown into confusion.

Examples of such confusion are everywhere. A man may hold loose views about the Bible, the atonement, the resurrection of Christ, and yet remain in the Methodist or Baptist ministry, not to mention others: but if a Methodist minister were to insist on baptism by immersion, or a Baptist minister to sprinkle instead of immerse, he would be disqualified at once! The same sort of thing applies to particular forms of administration. Thus rites and forms are given more importance than basic doctrines! Can we wonder at the blight on modern Protestantism?

Let it be said again that when we thus speak we are making no mere plea for intellectual unity on non-essentials. This question of our attitude to the Bible is one of life and death for the

Protestant cause. The first and most basal of all questions in theology is: "Has God spoken?" Until the rise of the German schools of the "Higher Criticism" Protestantism unitedly answered "Yes, in a unique, authoritative, final way through the inspired Scriptures, and supremely in His incarnate Son" (and let us ever realize that we owe our knowledge, even of the *living* Word, to the *written* word!).

When are the sons of Levi going to restore the ark to the place of supreme deference in the sanctuary? There will never be an end to our present ineffectuality until that happens. Revival will never break upon us while our attitude to the word of God is one of doubt instead of faith. Come, brethren, let us restore the ark! Let us restore the ark! Then, once again will the "glory of the Lord" fill the house! Then, also, we verily believe, our rulers and people will bow to the authority and saving-power of our message.

> This is the greatest book on earth;
>   Unparalleled it stands;
> Its author God, its truth divine,
> Inspired in every page and line,
>   Tho' writ with human hands.
>
> This is the volume of the Cross;
>   Its saving truth is sure;
> Its doctrine pure, its history true,
> Its Gospel old, yet ever new,
>   Shall evermore endure.

THE "UNPARDONABLE SIN"

—Matthew xii. 32

THE "UNPARDONABLE SIN"

"But whosoever speaketh against the Holy Spirit, it shall not be forgiven him, neither in this age, neither in the age to come." Matt. xii. 32.

THESE words of our Lord Jesus may well cause us astonishment. They mark the one awesome exception in the Gospel offer of universal pardon. All sins may be forgiven—except one!

The Gospel comes to us proclaiming that where human sin has abounded divine grace has "much more" abounded. It tells us that "all manner of sin and blasphemy" may be "forgiven unto men," through the mediatorial self-sacrifice of the Lord Jesus on Calvary. And, indeed, we know, both from the pages of Holy Writ and from the experience of redeemed sinners themselves, that the most monstrous sins *have* been thus forgiven to men. What, then, can be this fearful exception, this sin for which there is *no* forgiveness? We may well ask the question with solemnized concentration.

There are other reasons, too, why we ought to examine this matter carefully. Men and women under deep conviction for sin have suffered sheer torture of despair, assuming that they were beyond salvation through having committed the unpardonable sin, when in reality they had never come anywhere near committing it. Moreover, we ought to know what this unforgivable sin is so that we may shun it, and warn others against committing it. There is much vagueness as to what it really is, even among Christian believers.

So far as we know, our Lord only once spoke of the unpardonable sin; but His words and the incident which called them forth are recorded three times over for us, with slight variations, that is, by Matthew and Mark and Luke respectively. The passages are Matthew xii. 22–37; Mark iii. 22–30; Luke xi. 14–23. Matthew's is the most detailed account, and we ought to read carefully again what he says.

"Then was brought unto Him one possessed with a demon, blind and dumb; and He healed him, insomuch that the blind and dumb both spake and saw. And all the people were amazed and said, Is not this the Son of David?

"But when the Pharisees heard it they said, This fellow doth not cast out demons, but by Beelzebub, the prince of the demons. And Jesus knew their thoughts, and said unto them, Every kingdom divided against itself is brought to desolation, and every city or house divided against itself shall not stand; and if Satan cast out Satan he is divided against himself; how shall then his kingdom stand? And if I by Beelzebub cast out demons, by whom do your children cast them out? Therefore they shall be your judges. But if I cast out demons by the Spirit of God, then the kingdom of God is come unto you. Or else how can one enter into a strong man's house and spoil his goods except he first bind the strong man? and then he will spoil his house.

"He that is not with Me is against Me, and he that gathereth not with Me scattereth abroad. Wherefore I say unto you: All manner of sin and blasphemy shall be forgiven unto men; but the blasphemy against the Holy Spirit shall not be forgiven unto men. And whosoever speaketh a word against the Son of Man, it shall be forgiven him; but whosoever speaketh against the Holy Spirit, it shall not be forgiven him, neither in this age, neither in the age to come. Either make the tree good, and his fruit good; or else make the tree corrupt, and his fruit corrupt; for the tree is known by his fruit" (22–33).

Three questions are raised, and at the same time implicitly answered, by this passage—(1) What *is* the unpardonable sin? (2) Why is it unpardonable? (3) How does it relate to ourselves?

1. WHAT IS THE UNPARDONABLE SIN?

First, then, what *is* this unpardonable sin about which so much has been written, and which many have tried to explain away, and about which so many have been anxiously puzzled?

The first thing that strikes us is that the persons who were warned as being either guilty of committing the unpardonable sin or else in danger of committing it, were *very religious persons.* They were the "Pharisees," the most punctilious of all the Jewish religious sects, and the "scribes" (Mark iii. 22), who were the literary experts of the day in the sacred Scriptures! This is startling, and it begins to tell us right away what the unpardonable sin is *not.*

It is not any one particular, isolated sin of excessive vulgarity, impurity, or criminality, such as drunken debauchery, fornication, or murder; nor is it even a long-continued course of such "riotous living" and violence.

Most or all of these Pharisees and scribes could have said about the ten commandments just what the rich young ruler said to our Lord Jesus, in Mark x. 20, "All these have I observed from my youth." So far as outward morality was concerned, they each wore the "white flower of a blameless life." Yet these were the men whom Jesus warned as being almost, if not actually guilty of committing the unpardonable sin!

The next thing that strikes us is that the unpardonable sin is clearly some form of *sin against the Holy Spirit.* "Whosoever speaketh against the Holy Spirit, it shall not be forgiven him, neither in this age, neither in the age to come." Probably none of those who heard these words fall from the lips of Jesus would think of the Holy Spirit as a *Person* in the Godhead, distinct from the Father, any more than they recognized in Jesus Christ the incarnate *second* Person of the divine Triunity. They would think of the Holy Spirit as an influence exercised by God upon men. Their monotheism was unitarian, not trinitarian. The full revelation of God as a Triunity only breaks upon us as the pages of the New Testament proceed. But Jesus Himself knew the personalness of the Holy Spirit, and as we now look back on His words in the light of fuller revelation, we can see how even then His words practically *implied* the Holy Spirit's personality. The fact that our Lord's hearers did not apprehend the personalness of the Holy Spirit does not make our Lord's words any less solemn, but rather more so, for it indicates that we may commit the unpardonable sin against the Holy Spirit without even knowing that He *is* a person!

But now, going a step further, we cannot fail to see that the focus-point of our Lord's words is that this unpardonable sin is *the sin of "blasphemy"* against the Holy Spirit. Note the words in verse 31 again: "All manner of sin and blasphemy shall be forgiven unto men; but the blasphemy against the Holy Spirit shall not be forgiven." What is blasphemy? It is speaking in such a way as vilifies or insults or otherwise outrages God. In what way, then, were those old-time scribes and Pharisees outraging God? We are not left in any doubt. Note the little word "the" in our Lord's solemn warning—"But *the* blasphemy against the Holy Spirit. . . ." Why does He say "*the* blasphemy"? It is because He means the particular kind of blasphemy just uttered by these religious hypocrites, viz., "This fellow doth not cast out demons, but by Beelzebub the prince of the demons." Undoubtedly, then, this form of blasphemy against the Holy Spirit which is the unpardonable sin, is *the ascribing of the Holy Spirit's gracious and holy activities to the devil himself.* It is saying that the works of God's Spirit are the works of Satan.

But as soon as we see this clearly, that the unpardonable sin is the blasphemy of ascribing to the devil the works of the Holy Spirit, we are carried yet a step further by the context, and we can see *why* this blasphemy on the part of the scribes and Pharisees was so terrible. The factor which made it unpardonable was its being *intelligent, knowing, wilful and determined.* Had their sinister libel on the Holy Spirit been uttered ignorantly and unknowingly, it would at once have been pardonable. Paul the Apostle committed this sin of blasphemy before his conversion, so vitriolic was his hatred of the Nazarene and His followers; yet he was pardoned because he did it in ignorance. He himself says, in writing to Timothy: "I thank Christ Jesus our Lord who hath enabled me, for that He counted me faithful, putting me into the ministry, who was before a *blasphemer* and a persecutor; but I obtained mercy because I did it *ignorantly* in unbelief."

There was no such blasphemy in ignorance, however, on the part of the scribes and Pharisees in Matthew xii, whom our Lord warned of the unpardonable sin. The context makes this conclusively plain. That the beneficent miracles which our Lord was working were of the Holy Spirit was immediately perceptible even to common intelligence, so that the ordinary people spontaneously exclaimed, "Is not this the Son of David?" They knew at once that the works being done by Jesus were such as the prophets had foretold would be done by the Spirit of Jehovah through the coming Messiah. And besides being perceptible to common intelligence, it was a matter of patent argumentative demonstration. There was the *a priori* argument, "If Satan cast out Satan, how shall his kingdom stand?" And there was the *argumentum ad hominem*, "If I by Beelzebub cast out demons, by whom do your own sons (or disciples) cast them out?" There was no logical escape from our Lord's conclusion, "If I cast out demons by the Spirit of God, then the kingdom of God is come unto you." No, there was no escape, and these Pharisees knew it; yet they intelligently, knowingly, wilfully and determinedly alleged that what the Holy Spirit of God was doing was of the devil! What awful blasphemy, then, it was!

This leads us to one further and very striking point in the context. Look at verse 32 again: "And whosoever speaketh a word against *the Son of Man*, it shall be forgiven him; but whosoever speaketh against *the Holy Spirit*, it shall not be forgiven." Why was blasphemy against the Holy Spirit so much worse than blasphemy against Christ? Are they not both Persons of the Godhead, eternally co-equal? Yes; but here, in Matthew xii, the contrast is not between blaspheming one or other of the Persons of the Godhead as such (for as we have already noted, these people as yet neither understood the Holy Spirit to be a *Person* nor Christ Jesus to be the *second* Person of the Trinity). No, the contrast is that of blasphemy against Christ as "Son of *Man*," in His earthly work and under earthly conditions, the Christ whom they saw but did not understand, versus blasphemy against *God Himself*.

Therefore, now that our Lord Jesus has lived and taught and wrought and died and risen and ascended and poured out the Holy Spirit, now that it is demonstrated and known that He is very God, co-equal and co-eternal with the ever-blessed Father and the Holy Spirit, it is equally the unpardonable sin to ascribe *His* works to the devil, for that is now just as clearly blaspheming *God* as was the blasphemy of the old-time Pharisees against the Holy Spirit. To know that a work is of God, whether it be a work of the *Son* of God or a work of the *Spirit* of God, and to attribute it to the devil—*that is the unpardonable sin.*

2. WHY IS IT UNPARDONABLE?

But now the second of the three questions prompted by our text presses itself upon us: *Why* is this sin of blasphemy against the Spirit of God and of Christ unpardonable?

The first reason seems to be that this sin is not any one sin committed and then repented of, but *a fixed attitude of mind and heart*. It is not even a long-continued course of sin such as godless prodigals indulge in when they "waste their substance in riotous living," for that kind of sinning is a giving way to the lower appetites, rather than the product of a hard-set, intelligent attitude of defiance to God's Spirit. Men have gone to uttermost depths of depravity in fleshly ways, have wrecked their own lives and brought heart-break into the lives of others, yet later they have known contrition and have become saved in Christ. One has only to read the records of movements like the Salvation Army to know this; or one need only turn to 1 Corinthians vi. 9–11, and read Paul's "such were some of you."

Thank God, divine grace can reach down, and *does* reach down to the most sunken and debased among earth's profligates. But all that sort of sinning is sharply different from this form of sin which the scribes and Pharisees in Matthew xii were guilty, or almost guilty, of committing. Theirs was no sinning through fleshly weakness or spiritual ignorance; it was a set attitude of mind and heart against the true light, a knowing, determined closing of the soul's window against the light of divine truth, so that the shining of pardoning love simply could not break through. Their sin was unpardonable because it *precluded* pardon.

This, however, as we are quick to appreciate, provokes the further question: But *why* did even *that* form of sin preclude forgiveness? Could not these men have repented of that attitude of heart and mind, just as the prodigal in the parable repented of his "riotous living," and as thousands of others in real life have repented of their sin? The answer is, that if these Pharisees had indeed reached the point of unpardonableness, their sin precluded pardon because it precluded *repentance*.

Let us speak clearly but warily here. Our Lord does not say that these men either *had* or had *not* committed their sin to the degree where it made pardon impossible, but for the sake of clearness and definiteness here, let us momentarily suppose that they *had*. What then? Why, this: it means that their hard, knowing, evil attitude of refusing the true light of God rather than admit themselves in the wrong, had now reached such a state of fixity in them that the very *capacity* for repentence had become destroyed.

Mark well then: the unpardonable sin is a state of sin which precludes pardon *because it precludes repentance*. That such a point can be reached is definitely a fact. Men can allow and foster within themselves a process of hard refusal toward God which eventually becomes their master, and destroys the possibility of repentance. Men cannot repent merely at will. A minister acquaintance of mine told me of an awful death-bed visit he had been called upon to make. The dying man was writhing and struggling and striking the air in a piteously futile effort to fight death off. He was in stark terror at the thought of death and the dread Beyond. He eventually died demented; but both before and after his brain gave way he would periodically groan or wail, "I said I would repent before I died; but it won't come; it won't come! I *can't* repent!"

Yes, such a point can be reached, where the very capacity for repentance is destroyed. And where there is no more repentance there is no more pardon. That is why the unpardonable sin *is* unpardonable. It is not just any one act of sin. It is not even a prolonged series of sins. It is a *state of heart and mind reached by a process*, a process of sinful refusal towards God and divine truth, such as we have described.

On the ground of our Lord's atoning self-sacrifice for sinful man, God can forgive any sin, however vile and black it may be. He can forgive a prolonged series of such sins, where there is contrition. But this condition of soul in which the very capability of repentance is destroyed, *cannot* be forgiven, any more than a physician can forgive atrophy or pardon a cancer.

So, then, the sin that has no forgiveness is a fixed state after a long process of knowing opposition to the Spirit of God, and of hatred to His work. It is the Holy Spirit who convicts "of sin, and of righteousness, and of judgment." It is He who makes real to the human heart, the love of God in Christ Jesus toward sinful men. It is He who begets in the human heart, "love, joy, peace, longsuffering, gentleness, goodness, faith, meekness, temperance," and every godly virtue. The awful thing is that men can know these things and yet learn to hate them. It is then that the process begins which ends at last in complete alienation from God, and the sin which can never be forgiven. The light which was once in a man can "become darkness"; and then, as our Lord says, "How great is that darkness!" The man who has really reached that point will never turn. He will continue to hate the light for ever. He will be like the demons who "believe and tremble" (Jas. ii. 19) but do not *repent* because they *cannot* repent. There can come a point, the culmination of a process, where God must say, in effect, what was said in a national sense of the ten-tribed Israel kingdom long ago, through the prophet Hosea, "Ephraim is joined to idols: *let him alone.*" When that point is reached, further inter-ference in grace is thwarted. The sun which melts the wax *hardens* the clay. "Let him alone"—they are awful words. *There* is the unpardonable sin. There can be no more forgiveness, for there is left no more capability of repentance.

In the Scriptures there are three striking and awesome examples of this process which ends in the unpardonable sin. Notably enough, they are three kings—Pharaoh, Saul, Herod.

Take *Pharaoh* (Exod. i–xiv). We see from the first that he was a wicked man, in his cruel devices to inflict suffering on the Israelites. To this man there was given, by successive "plagues," such a demonstration of the power of the true God, that there could be no doubt left in his own mind that it *was* indeed the true God who was now saying, "Let My people go." Both Pharaoh and his men were forced to see this. Yet Pharaoh determined to defy God.

It might seem preposterous that a mere *man* could knowingly dare to do this; but read the following lines from the late F. B. Meyer:

"In order to appreciate the audacity of the demand, we must remember the unbridled power and authority which were claimed by the Egyptian monarchs. Each Pharaoh was the child of the sun. He is depicted as fondled by the greatest gods, and sitting with them in the recesses of their temples to receive worship equal to their own. 'By the life of Pharaoh,' was the supreme oath. Without Pharaoh could no man lift up his hand or foot in all the land of Egypt. For him great Egypt existed. For him all other men lived, suffered, and died. For him the mighty Nile flowed from its unexplored fountains to fructify the soil. For him vast armies of priests, and magicians, and courtiers, wrought and ministered. From his superb throne he looked down on the wretched crowds of subject peoples, careless of their miseries. What were their tears and groans, and the wail of their bondage, but a fitting sacrifice to be offered to his exalted majesty! In addition, the present monarch had recently, through his generals, achieved certain great victories; and these successes had greatly enhanced his arrogant pride, so that it was in a paroxysm of supercilious scorn that he answered the Divine demand: 'Who is the Lord, that I should obey His voice, to let Israel go? I know not the Lord, neither will I let Israel go.'

"The point of the reply lies in that word *obey*. He saw that these men did not present him with a request, but with a mandate from One of greater authority than himself. This stung him to the quick. He also was a god. Who was this other God, stronger than himself, who dared to issue such a summons! A God of whose existence till that moment he had been unaware! The God of a parcel of slaves! How dare they speak of their paltry Deity in his presence, and in the midst of priests, courtiers, and high officers of state!"

This was the proud, vain, wicked man who set himself to resist God. In so doing he started the deadly process in his own soul which leads at last to the unpardonable sin. Eighteen times we are told that Pharaoh's heart was "hardened" in refusal. In about half of these the hardening is attributed to God, and in the other half to Pharaoh himself. That is significant. It shows the reciprocal activity of God in relation to such impenitence. To the man who thus defiantly hardens himself God says, "Ye shall *be* hardened." We have the same in our Lord's lament over Jerusalem—"How often *would* I . . . Ye would *not* . . . Ye *shall* not."

There are those who have found difficulty in the fact that *God* is said to have hardened Pharaoh's heart. But the whole contest between God and Pharaoh must be interpreted by what God said to Moses before the contest started: "The king of Egypt *will not* . . ." The will was already set. The heart was already hard. God only hardened him further inasmuch as the plagues forced Pharaoh to an issue which *crystallised* his sin. The outcome is well enough known.

A milder, but much more pathetic case, is that of *Saul, first king of Israel*. His career runs in three phases—his early promise, his later decline, his final failure. He starts out with a striking physical superiority, highly commendable traits of disposition, special spiritual equipment by the Holy Spirit, a band of godly men around him, and that trusty adviser, Samuel the prophet.

But self-will and resistance to God more and more gain the upper hand in his life. He gives way to irreverent presumption in violating the priest's prerogative (1 Sam. xiii). Then he rashly disobeys God (xiv). Then he both disobeys God and lies to Samuel (xv). Then he grieves away the Spirit of God, and gives way to a petty jealousy of David until it becomes a fiendish malice, so that three times he tries to kill him, and hunts him like "a partridge on the mountains" for months on end! More and more he has said "No" to the Spirit of God; and more and more the Spirit of God leaves him; until at length he groans, "God is departed from me and answereth me no more, neither by prophets nor by dreams." And the man who started out with such fair promise ends by consulting the witch of Endor and then committing suicide!

We do not say that Saul actually reached that point which our Lord calls the unpardonable sin; but he certainly illustrates the process which leads to it.

Finally, take *King Herod* the Tetrarch. These are the salient facts about him spiritually. First, despite much sin, there was still the voice of God in his life, for in Mark vi. 20 we read: "Herod feared John (the Baptist), knowing that he was a just man and a holy, and observed him; and when he heard him he did many things, hearing him gladly." Herod, however, had developed an infatuation for Herodias, his brother Philip's wife, and wanted to marry her unlawfully. Herod must now either listen to the voice of God through John, or the voice of sin through Herodias. He made his choice. He put John in prison and married Herodias (verses 17–19). Thus, as he thought, he had conveniently rid himself of the troublesome voice of God.

Now mark the process which is going on. In Luke iii. 19, 20, where the same incident is referred to, Luke speaks of "all the evils which Herod had done," and says that he "*Added* yet this above all, that he shut up John in prison." Later on he went the extreme length of beheading John to please Herodias (Mark vi. 27). Even then the voice of God through conscience was not altogether silenced. When the fame of Jesus spread abroad, Herod guiltily exclaimed, "This is John the Baptist; he is risen from the dead!" Later on we read of his purposing to kill Jesus also (Luke xiii. 31). At last Jesus is brought before Herod, having been sent there by Pilate on the morning of the crucifixion. And *now* what happens? Luke xxiii. 9 tells us that Herod "questioned with Him in many words," but that Jesus "answered him *nothing*." The voice of God which had been knowingly and systematically silenced in his life *will not speak any more!* In his rage and frustration Herod now has Jesus "set at naught" by his soldiers, and "mocked"; but Jesus remains mute. The voice of God speaks no more. The man who *would* not *shall* not! "Ephraim is joined to idols: let him alone"! Such is the unpardonable sin; and such is the process leading to it.

3. HOW DOES IT RELATE TO OURSELVES?

We come to our third question: How does our Lord's warning relate to ourselves?

In the first place, let us be assured that *the unpardonable sin can really be committed.* Our Lord's solemn words were no mere warning against a fiction. The unpardonable sin can be, and has been committed. *Satan* presumably has committed it. In all the millenniums of his sinning, from his first sin until now, Satan has never once committed a sin through ignorance, or because he was tempted to it. He has always sinned of himself, knowing with a more-than-human intelligence that he was

sinning against the light and love of God. He has sinned in
such a way and to such a point that he is incapable of repentance. There can be no forgiveness for him, but only the lake
of fire.

Likewise, the *fallen angels* seem to have perpetrated that sin
which has no forgiveness. The angels are spirit-beings. There
is no such thing as heredity among them. Each fallen angel
sinned of himself, in complete independence, absolutely of his
own will, without any inward bias to wrong, and knowing that
it was intelligent rebellion against God. There has been begotten
in them a state of implacable impenitence. There can be no
forgiveness, but only Gehenna.

It looks as though Pharaoh and perhaps Herod *may* have
committed the unpardonable sin. It is possible, too, that some
of the religious hypocrites of our Lord's day came very near
to it, for they had gone so far as to say, with knowing and
deliberate hypocrisy, that the Holy Spirit's gracious ministries
were the doings of the devil; and Jesus said to certain of them,
"Ye are of your father, the devil"!

Coming down to modern times, we find ourselves asking
whether a man like Adolf Hitler committed the unpardonable
sin. There seems to have been the same characteristic process
in him; the systematic stifling of conscience, the ever-increasing
lying and deceiving, until the moral sense is utterly perverted;
black is white, and wrong is right, and evil is good, and the
devil is God! And, if we are right in specially relating Psalm ii
to the end-period of this present age, it looks as though ruling-
powers are going to commit something like the unpardonable
sin as a prelude to Armageddon.

Yes, the unpardonable sin may be committed.

But we may make another application of this to ourselves
which is genuinely comforting. It is this: those who are troubled
and concerned lest they have committed the unpardonable sin,
definitely have *not* committed it. Their anxious disturbedness
about it is in itself the evidence that they have not done so.
No Christian believer has committed it, whatever deep back-
sliding there may have been. No sincere seeker after God has
committed it, however grievous may have been the sin of past
years. No sinner, convicted of his sin, fearing the judgment to

come, seeking to know the way of salvation, and longing to live a better life, has committed it. This is certainly true, for all such emotions and desires and contrition in the human heart are the work of the Holy Spirit, and are therefore proof from God Himself that the unpardonable sin has not been committed.

How Satan uses this fear of having committed the unpardonable sin to distress backslidden Christians and seekers after salvation! To all such we say: Have no fear; you have *not* committed it. The gracious Spirit Himself is at work in your heart. He is saying to you the *other* part of our text—"All manner of sin and blasphemy shall be forgiven unto men"; and that includes all *yours* !

The late Dr. G. Campbell Morgan says: "The sin referred to cannot be committed during probation. It is not the sin of an hour. It is not the sin of an act. It is the sin of an attitude, definitely taken, and persistently maintained, to the end of the period of probation. That period never ends until man crosses the boundary between this life and the life that lies beyond. We are living in the day of grace; and in that day the Spirit never abandons a man."

I believe that in 999,000 cases out of every million those words are right. I believe that the only man whom God finally abandons is the man who finally abandons God. Let sincere hearts be convinced and comforted.

But we go on to make just one more brief application to ourselves. That is, we ought to guard with never-abating vigilance against *even the beginnings* of that process which leads to the unpardonable sin.

Almost always it begins in one or other of three ways—by postponing, or by presuming, or by pretending.

Through the inward convicting of the Holy Spirit, souls are awakened to a concern about their eternal salvation. They are convinced as to the truth of the Gospel and the power of Jesus to save them. They know what they ought to do, but they *postpone*, until gradually the sense of urgency subsides. Where this sort of thing is repeated, the postponing grows easier each time, for the soul's capability of right reaction is being vitiated; and as the process confirms itself, the soul gradually seals its own doom in a chronic incapacity for repentance.

E

In other cases souls *presume* on God. They fully intend to be saved, but they presume to choose their own time, stupidly ignoring that conviction and conversion, repentance and regeneration are the Holy Spirit's work in the heart, not just the self-willings of human beings themselves.

In still other cases the process leading to the unpardonable sin is engendered by *pretending*, by being unreal with God and with one's own conscience, by affecting to be saved when in reality the heart is unchanged and still hugs sin, by saying in effect, "Oh yes, I believe in the Gospel, so I must be all right, and I can easily dodge having to renounce this and that and the other thing". One can practise this fatal folly of deception until the heart really comes to think a thing is true even though at first it knew well enough that it was false. Black is white and white is black, and the heart is a lie to itself!

I suppose there *are* cases where from the beginning there is a rejecting, a refusing, a rebelling; but in most cases the evil process begins more gently, simply as a postponing or a presuming or a pretending; and it is almost invariably because the heart will not tear itself away from its pet indulgences. Oh, may we put far from us all such foolish toying about with divine and eternal realities, and live to the glory of God by a genuine consecratedness to the dear Saviour!

THE SUICIDE OF JUDAS

—Matthew xxvii. 3–10
Acts i. 18, 19.

THE SUICIDE OF JUDAS

It is not easy to preach on Judas. Somehow, whenever we think of him we feel a heart-shudder. Of all distinguishments the ugliest, to have been the false friend and Satan-possessed betrayer of the holy Son of God! It is some little relief to know that as soon as he saw the result of his betrayal, he "repented himself" and flung the wretched blood-money at the feet of the religious hypocrites who had bribed him. And his very suicide, wrong as suicide is, confirms to us the reality of his utter remorse, even though perhaps in that darkened heart there was no real repentance.

But in connection with Judas's suicide and the blood-money there arises a strange-seeming problem which (we find) has perplexed many. It is the seeming contradiction between Matthew's account, in Matthew xxvii. 3–10, and that of Peter recorded in Acts i. 18, 19.

Some years ago we used to preach at a certain open-air meeting in the heart of a busy city; and invariably, if we invited questions, there was a pleasant-faced elderly man, a rank ridiculer of the Gospel, who used to pipe out sarcastically: "The Bible has big blunders in it, and you can't deny it. It contradicts itself. In Matthew it says that Judas went and hanged himself, and that the priests bought a field with the thirty pieces of silver. In Acts it says that it was Judas himself, not the priests, who bought the field, and that instead of hanging himself he fell headlong and his inside fell out. How can you get over that? You *can't* get over it!"

Yes, how do we get over *that*? Only a few weeks ago a Christian leader who now helps at that same open-air meeting was telling me that our pleasant-faced free-thinker still hovers round and pipes out his invincible little disprover of the Bible. However, he has now got his answer. We were appealed to by this Christian worker, and asked if *we* could supply an answer. This sent us back to the Scripture; and, as we carefully examined the two accounts in Matthew and Acts respectively, we came to see that there is a solution as clear as noon-day and final as a mathematical demonstration.

Let us set down the two accounts, then, one after the other, and compare them carefully. This is what Matthew says, in chapter xxvii, verses 3 to 10:

"Then Judas, which had betrayed Him, when he saw that He was condemned, repented himself, and brought again the thirty pieces of silver to the chief priests and elders, saying: I have sinned in that I have betrayed the innocent blood. And they said: What is that to us? See thou to that. And he cast down the pieces of silver in the temple, and departed, and went and hanged himself.

"And the chief priests took the silver pieces, and said: It is not lawful for to put them into the treasury, because it is the price of blood. And they took counsel, and bought with them the potter's field, to bury strangers in. Wherefore that field was called, The Field of Blood, unto this day.

"Then was fulfilled that which was spoken by Jeremy the prophet, saying: And they took the thirty pieces of silver, the price of him that was valued, whom they of the children of Israel did value, and gave them for the potter's field, as the Lord appointed me."

And now, this is what Peter is reported as saying, in the Acts of the Apostles, the first chapter, verses 19 and 20:

"Now this man (Judas) purchased a field with the reward of iniquity; and falling headlong, he burst asunder in the midst, and all his bowels gushed out. And it was known unto all the dwellers at Jerusalem, insomuch as that field is called in their proper tongue, Aceldama, that is to say, The Field of Blood.

Now there are really *three* problems here: (1) the seeming discrepancy as to who bought the field, Judas or the priests; (2) the seeming contradiction as to the way Judas met his death; (3) the seeming error as to which Old Testament prophecy is supposed to have been fulfilled by it. Take these in order.

1. THE PROBLEM OF THE PURCHASE

First, then, who bought the "field"? Matthew says, "*They* (the priests) took counsel, and bought the potter's field." Peter says, "*This man* (Judas) purchased a field." And in both Matthew and Acts, the field becomes known as the "field of blood."

The answer is that both the priests *and* Judas were the purchasers! They both purchased; and they purchased independently of each other! Does that seem unbelievable? Well, it is the truth; and it will quickly become intelligible when we explain that the "field" in Matthew xxvii is not the same as the "field" in Acts i; and the "buying" in Matthew is not the same as the "purchasing" in Acts; and the time when the priests bought is different from the time when Judas purchased. In other words, Matthew's account and that in the Acts refer to *two different transactions*!

Does that come as a surprise? Then let us examine the two accounts and verify it. When Matthew says that the chief priests bought a "field," the Greek word is *agros*, which truly enough means a field in our own usual sense of the word; but when Peter, in Acts i, says that Judas himself purchased a "field," the Greek word is *chōrion*, which means a farm or what we might now call "a smallholding." The two are definitely different.

But further, not only are the two nouns thus different, the two verbs of acquirement are also different. In Matthew xxvii the verb translated as "bought" is *agorazō*, and means to buy in the open market. But in Acts i the word translated as "purchased" is *ktaomai* (from *ktema*, a possession), and means to become possessed of, to acquire for one's own self. The Revised Version rightly recognises this difference by translating it as "obtained."

But now, still further, not only are the two nouns and the two verbs different, but the two occasions of purchase are different. This is necessarily so in view of the following facts.

First, Judas's "purchase" was made before ever he received those thirty pieces of silver. It *must* have been, as a little reflection shows, and may probably have been made a considerable space of time before. In Matthew xxvi. 2, we find our Lord

saying, "Ye know that after *two days* is the feast of the Passover" (see also Mark xiv. 1). On the evening of that day there
is the "supper" at Bethany (see Matt. xxvi. 6–13; Mark xiv. 3–9;
John xii. 2–8). At this supper our Lord rebukes Judas for his
hypocritical criticism of Mary and her alabaster box of ointment
(John xii. 4–8). It is immediately after this supper and rebuke
that Judas goes to the chief priests (see Matt. xxvi. 14; Mark
xiv. 10; John xii. 4).

Now this was the Wednesday night. On the Thursday night
our Lord was arrested in Gethsemane. Early the next morning,
Friday, Judas returned to the chief priests and flung the money
at their feet. Therefore, even supposing Judas had received
the thirty pieces of silver right away on the Wednesday evening,
there was only the one day between then and the Friday morning
in which he could have looked round and decided oñ the place
he wanted to purchase, and have seen the owner and gone through
all the preliminaries to such a conveyance of land. And even
on that one day, as we know, he was for part of the time with
our Lord and the disciples (Matt. xxvi. 17–25).

This alone makes it highly improbable that Judas could have
bought a "field" with that thirty pieces of silver. But there
are two other factors which settle the matter conclusively. Judas
did *not* receive the money on his *first* visit to the chief priests.
They only promised it to him then! In Luke xxii. 5 we read:
"And they (the chief priests) were glad, and *covenanted* to give
him money." The money would only be actually given him
when the betrayal was successfully expedited—an arrangement
just such as we would expect on the part of men who were as
wily as they were wicked. And if Judas only received the money
on the *Thursday* night, then he certainly could not have bought
a "field" with it by Friday morning.

But the final proof, of course, that Judas had made no such
purchase at that time is seen in the fact that on the Friday
morning he still *had* the thirty pieces of silver in his possession,
and flung them back at the men who had hired him.

Therefore, the "purchase" by Judas, referred to in Acts i,
must certainly have been made some time *before* the betrayal
and crucifixion of our Lord; whereas the buying of the "field"
by the chief priests was certainly *after* the crucifixion. "And

the chief priests took the silver pieces, and said: It is not lawful for to put them into the treasury, because it is the price of blood. And *they took counsel*, and bought with them the potter's field to bury strangers in." Obviously that was no hurried buying on the actual Friday of the crucifixion. It happened some time afterward.

So then, the two purchasings in Matthew xxvii and Acts i, respectively, are clearly *not* one and the same. The one is a "field"; the other is a "farm." The one is bought in the open market; the other is acquired by private purchase. The one is by the chief priests some time *after* the crucifixion; the other is by Judas, some time *before* the crucifixion.

2. THE PROBLEM OF THE SUICIDE

The second problem is a very unpleasant one to discuss; but fortunately it can be disposed of quite briefly. *Where* and *how* did Judas commit suicide? Matthew simply says, "He went and hanged himself." Peter, in Acts i, says, "Now this man purchased a field (a smallholding) with the reward of iniquity; and falling headlong, he burst asunder, and all his bowels gushed out."

Now because the "field" in Matthew xxvii. 7, and the "smallholding" in Acts i. 18 have been looked upon as one and the same, it has been generally assumed that Judas hanged himself in the field bought by the chief priests, and that it was for this reason that the field became called "the field of blood" (Matt. xxvii. 8). But here again, a little reflection will show that Judas simply could not have hanged himself in the field which the chief priests bought.

In the first place, when Judas hanged himself, the priests had not then bought the field. In the second place, if Judas *had* hanged himself in that field, he could not have known beforehand that it was the field which the chief priests were going to decide on buying; it could only have been by the sheerest coincidence. But, in the third place, if Judas *had* hanged himself in that field, the chief priests would never have bought it at all, for it would have been considered accursed.

But it may be asked: Do not Matthew xxvii. 8 and Acts i. 18 both say that the place became known as "the field of blood"?

The answer is that they do *not*. Reflect again. We have already shown that the word "field," in Matthew, is *agros*, and that in Acts it is *chōrion*. So is it with that expression, "the field of blood." In Matthew xxvii it is "the *agros* (or field) of blood." In Acts i it is the "*chōrion* (property or farmstead) of blood." It was at this place, his own dwelling or smallholding, that Judas committed suicide, and not in the field which the chief priests bought some time later. Both the *agros* which the chief priests "bought" and the *chōrion* which Judas had "purchased" became called places of "blood," but from two different connections. The "field," in Matthew xxvii, was called "the field of blood" because it was bought with the money given for the blood of *Jesus*. The "farm," in Acts i, was called "the property (or dwelling) of blood," because of the suicide committed there by *Judas*. The latter place was also called *Aceldama* (Acts i. 19), an Aramaic name by which the "field" in Matthew xxvii was *not* called, nor *could* have been called.

As for the *description* of Judas's suicide, a careful reading of the two statements in Matthew and Acts will now show that what may have seemed like contradiction is in reality confirmation. The Acts account simply amplifies Matthew's statement that Judas hanged himself. In Matthew we have it simply from the standpoint of the *priests*, that is, he simply left them and "went and hanged himself"; and they probably knew no more than that, nor bothered to enquire; and when they bought their "field" with the thirty pieces of silver, it did not become called "the field of blood" with any thought of Judas at all, but because the thirty pieces were the price given for the blood of *Jesus*.

But in Acts i we have it uttered from the more intimate knowledge of Judas's former comrades and fellow-disciples, and uttered frankly among themselves. They knew that he had committed his suicide in his own miserable bit of questionably acquired property which had subsequently become known as Aceldama. Judas certainly *had* gone and "hanged himself," as the Matthew account says; but here, in Acts i, we get the fuller picture. The wretched man makes his way to this "place" which he had "purchased" for himself, probably with money stolen from the "bag" (John xii. 6), and hangs himself in some quiet, out-of-the-way corner there. Thus, the corpse hangs for some time undiscovered, and then, of its own weight, falls, rupturing the walls of the stomach, with the result described by Peter in Acts i.

But it may still be asked: Does it not say in Acts i that Judas purchased that *chōrion* with "the reward of iniquity"? And does not "the reward of iniquity" mean the thirty pieces of silver? The answer is that the expression "the reward of iniquity" does *not* refer to the thirty pieces of silver. It is simply a Hebrew idiom corresponding to expressions of our own, such as "money ill-got," or "ill-gotten gain." It refers, not to the thirty pieces of silver, but to the *thieving* of Judas mentioned in John xii. 6. Judas had purchased his "smallholding" with fraudulently appropriated money.

3. THE PROBLEM OF THE FULFILMENT

We come now to the third of our problems in connection with this Judas incident. Matthew tells us how the chief priests "took counsel" and then used the thirty pieces of silver to buy "the potter's field," for burying "strangers" in. That is quite clear, and presents no difficulty; but Matthew then goes on to add that their doing so fulfilled a prophecy of Jeremiah, and *that*, as all careful readers of Scripture have felt, *does* create a problem; for there does not seem to be anything anywhere in the Book of Jeremiah which really resembles it. This is what Matthew says:

"And they took counsel, and bought with them the potter's field, to bury strangers in. Wherefore that field was called the field of blood unto this day.

"Then was fulfilled that which was spoken by Jeremy the prophet, saying: And they took the thirty pieces of silver, the price of him that was valued, whom they of the children of Israel did value."

Of course, the marginal reference in our English Bibles directs us to Jeremiah xviii. 1–4, but when we turn to that passage we find nothing at all about thirty pieces of silver or the purchasing of a field. The only connection seems to be in the fact that Jeremiah went down to "the *potter's* house." Later on in the Book of Jeremiah we certainly do find that Jeremiah bought a field. That is in chapter xxxii. But that was the field of Hanameel in Anathoth, and was bought for "*seventeen* shekels of silver." So even if we put the two chapters together, with the "potter" and the "field" and the "seventeen shekels of silver" all side by side, we are little if any nearer to Matthew's words.

When we turn to the prophet *Zechariah*, however, we find something which seems very much nearer our requirement. In Zechariah xi. 7–14, we find an actual, and at the same time symbolic, incident in which the prophet is "*priced*" (or "valued" as Matthew gives it), and a "*thirty pieces of silver*" which are cast for the "*potter*" in the "*house of Jehovah*." There certainly is correspondence here between Matthew and Zechariah:

"They took the thirty pieces of silver, the price of him that was valued . . ." (Matt. xxvii).

"They weighed thirty pieces of silver for the price of me . . ." (Zech. xi. 12).

Obviously, the passage in Zechariah is intendedly enigmatical, and there are certain details in which it does not seem quite to tally with Matthew's words. The chief of these is that in Matthew it is the *chief priests* who buy the potter's field with the thirty pieces of silver, whereas in Zechariah it is *the prophet himself* who casts them to the potter in the house of the Lord—though even in this we can readily see how the prophet's doing it himself may have been a typical foreshadowing of what both Judas and the chief priests did, namely, the "casting" of the money in the temple, and the taking of it "to the potter."

One thing is thus clear: In the Old Testament there is ample basis for the wording, "then was fulfilled," in Matthew xxviii. 9. But the problem still confronts us that it is *Jeremiah's* words which are said to have been fulfilled. What can we say to *that*?

When we think of some of the things which *have* been said about it by leading Christian scholars and commentators we cannot but feel shame. The devout and scholarly Alford, of all commentators, calls it a "slip of the pen" by Matthew! Bishop

Wordsworth says it is a mistake allowed by the Holy Spirit to teach us not to trouble ourselves as to who the writers were, but to receive *all* prophecy as direct from God! Augustine suggests that Matthew was only quoting "from memory"! Eusebius and others say that the passage was originally in Jeremiah, but that the Jews cut it out, though they cannot prove this. Bishop Lightfoot and others suggest that Matthew puts Jeremiah as representing the whole body of the prophets, but *why* Matthew should do so is hard to see. Perhaps we are getting nearer the truth in the view of Origen and some others, that the passage which Matthew refers to was in *another* writing of Jeremiah which became lost. Or we may be still nearer the truth in the suggestion put forward in Smith's Bible Dictionary, that some annotator wrote "Jeremiah" in the margin and that it thereby crept into the text.

Yet surely the first thing to note in Matthew xxviii. 9, is that Matthew does not say that Jeremiah had *written* anything about it at all! He says, "Then was fulfilled that which was SPOKEN by Jeremy the prophet . . ." Now in a number of places we find careful distinction made between that which is written and that which is spoken, as for instance our Lord's reference to Moses, in John v. 47, "If ye believe not his *writings*, how shall ye believe my *words*?" May it not well be that there were *sayings* of some of the prophets handed down at first orally, and then perhaps more permanently preserved in Jewish collections which were later destroyed in the awful tribulation and destruction which came upon Judaea? Is it not plain, for example; that in Matthew v, verses 21, 27, 31, 33, 38, 43, where our Lord uses the formula, "Ye have *heard* that *it was said*," He was referring to some well-known Jewish catechism then in use, and which perished long ago? Our Lord never refers to *the Scriptures themselves* in that way.

Perhaps we need say no more on this point. It is not one on which anyone can speak with absolute finality at the moment; but we have said enough to show that Matthew's reference to Jeremiah might be no problem at all if we had fuller information. Matthew may have been writing with a knowledge and a precision upon which we ourselves are quite incompetent to pass any critical judgment. We do not now possess all the data required for a final verdict. But so long as the word *"spoken"* remains different from the word *"written,"* just so long will Matthew's words remain invulnerable—"Then was fulfilled that which was SPOKEN by Jeremy the prophet. . . ."

JUDAS—A WARNING!

To all these studies in problem texts we have tried to give a pertinent practical turn. What is it that the tragedy of Judas says to us above all else? He is a warning to us. He warns us against the love of money. He shows us that the inordinate love of money (quite apart from the actual possession of it) degrades the heart, deadens the conscience, and may easily lead to the most diabolical betrayal of all that is best and purest and loveliest. It has happened again and again. Judas is the classical example of it.

"Judas is a warning to all who have to do with the handling of money—to men of trust and men of trade—to men of every class and every occupation. Nor forget, that, as a very little stimulated his rapacity, as petty thefts were all he could practise, so small resources and tiny gains may nurse and nourish the spirit of a fatal worldliness. Avarice is the disease of the poor as well as the rich; and heaven may be lost, not only by grasping at thousands of gold, but by striving to clutch a few pieces of silver. If there ever was a time when the example of Judas ought to be set up as a warning, when the lessons of his history appeared specially suitable, and most called for, it is the present time. A mad and unprincipled pursuit of gain is the evil genius —the demon of the age. You find it in all our towns and cities and villages, haunting every market and manufactory, every counting-house and shop. You find it flying about everywhere —penetrating into secret places, entering the parlour and the closet, whispering into the ears of men and women, tempting them to sacrifice honour and principle, and their own souls, for the sake of gratifying the love of acquisition. Could we command the statistics of spiritual crime, and classify the numbers that perish, and put them down under the head of the besetting sin to which their everlasting ruin was primarily attributable, we apprehend that a longer catalogue would be found in the column appropriated to the unbridled lust of gain, than in those distinguished by the names either of intemperance or of lust."

C. H. Spurgeon says: "Judas had the very closest intimacy with Christ in the days of his public ministry; he was so trusted by the Saviour that he kept the little treasury in which Christ put, when there were any, the excesses, the excessive gifts of charity; he was the treasurer of the little company, you know him—Judas. He had been with Jesus almost everywhere; he had been His familiar friend and acquaintance, and when he dipped the bread with Him in the sop, it was but an indication of the close association which had been preserved between the Divine Master and a creature unworthy of such privilege. Yet there was never such a child of perdition as Judas, the friend and acquaintance of Christ; never one sinks lower in the depths of Divine wrath, with so huge a millstone about his neck, as this man with whom Christ took such sweet counsel, and went to the house of God in company. The same sun ripens the corn and the poppies. This man was ripened in guilt by the same external process that ripens others in holiness."

Yes, indeed, Judas is a warning!

WHO WERE THOSE "SONS OF GOD"?

—Genesis vi. 1–4.

FOUR PROBLEM TEXTS INTERLINKED

"And it came to pass, when men began to multiply on the face of the earth, and daughters were born unto them, that the sons of God saw the daughters of men that they were fair; and they took them wives of all which they chose. And the Lord said: My Spirit shall not always strive with man, for that he also is flesh; yet his days shall be an hundred and twenty years. There were giants in the earth in those days: and also after that, when the sons of God came in unto the daughters of men, and they bare children to them, the same became mighty men which were of old, men of renown."—Genesis vi. 1–4.

"Christ also suffered for sins once, the righteous for the unrighteous, that He might bring us to God, being put to death in the flesh, but quickened in the spirit, in which also he went and preached unto the spirits in prison, which aforetime were disobedient, when the long-suffering of God waited in the days of Noah."—I. Peter iii. 18–20.

"God spared not the angels that sinned, but cast them down to hell, and delivered them into chains of darkness, to be reserved unto judgment."—II. Peter ii. 4.

"And the angels which kept not their first estate, but left their own habitation, He hath reserved in everlasting chains under darkness unto the judgment of the great day."—Jude 6.

NOTE.—We have thought it well to give more space to this final study because it involves not just one, but *four* problem texts, and because it brings so many interesting considerations under review. Moreover, the subject has been so complexified by the pens of rival expositors that to have dealt with it skimpingly here would have been worse than not tackling it at all.

J. S. B.

WHO WERE THOSE "SONS OF GOD"?

A QUARTETTE OF PROBLEM TEXTS

Genesis vi. 1–4; 1 Peter iii. 18–20; 2 Peter ii. 4; Jude 6

PERHAPS nothing has evoked more curiosity among students of Genesis than the reference to "the sons of God" in the opening verses of chapter vi. We are told that when men began to multiply on the earth, the "sons of God" saw the daughters of men that they were fair, and took themselves wives therefrom at will. Then it is added that the children who resulted from these unions became "mighty men" and "men of renown." We are also told that there were "giants" in the earth in those days. Who, then, were those "sons of God"? If they were just sons of Adam, why are they called "sons of God?" Or if they were not sons of Adam, were they some superior order of creature then alive? Were they, in fact, as many have held, the "angels which kept not their first estate, but left their own habitation" (Jude 6)?

Although it may not appear so at a glance, this question has such important bearings that it is well worth our while to attempt a really adequate answer.

WERE THE "SONS OF GOD" SINNING ANGELS?

The explanation that the "sons of God" in Genesis vi were angels, who thus left "their first estate," has had many and able advocates both in early times and in more recent days. We ourselves have been surprised at the number of persons we have met who hold this view. That able writer, Mr. G. H. Pember, strongly argues it in his book, *Earth's Earliest Ages*; and that resourceful though sometimes rather fanciful exegete, the late Dr. E. W. Bullinger, widely popularized it.

If what is recorded in Genesis vi was indeed a voluptuous invasion of angels upon earth's womankind, then it is a prodigy of history, opening up all manner of speculation. Are there adequate grounds on which to believe it?

I do not think the case for this theory can ever have been put more popularly than by Mr. Pember and Dr. Bullinger. What then are the arguments? To know this we must refer to *Earth's Earliest Ages*, by the former, and *How to Enjoy the Bible*, by the latter. In order to do justice to them, we are obliged to quote fairly fully. Mr. Pember writes as follows:

"A new and startling event burst upon the world, and fearfully accelerated the already rapid progress of evil. 'The sons of God saw the daughters of men that they were fair; and they took them wives of all which they chose' (Gen. vi. 4). These words are often explained to signify nothing more than the intermarriage of the descendants of Cain and Seth; but a careful examination of the passage will elicit a far deeper meaning.

"When *men*, we are told, began to multiply on the face of the earth, and daughters were born unto them, the sons of God saw the daughters of *men*. Now by 'men' in each case the whole human race is evidently signified, the descendants of Cain and Seth alike. Hence the 'sons of God' are plainly distinguished from the generation of Adam.

"Again, the expression 'sons of God (Elohim)' occurs but four times in other parts of the Old Testament, and is in each of these cases indisputably used of angelic beings.

"Twice in the beginning of the Book of Job we read of the sons of God presenting themselves before Him at stated times, and Satan also comes with them as being himself a son of God, though a fallen and rebellious one.

"For the term, sons of Elohim, the mighty Creator, seems to be confined to those who were directly created by the Divine hand, and not born of other beings of their own order. Hence in Luke's genealogy of our Lord, Adam is called a son of God (Luke iii. 38). And so also Christ is said to give to them that receive Him power to become the sons of God (John i. 12). For these are born again of the Spirit of God as to their inner man even in the present life. And at the resurrection they will be clothed with a spiritual body, a building of God (2 Cor. v. 1); so that they will then be in every respect equal to the angels, being altogether a new creation.

"The third repetition of the phrase occurs in a later chapter of Job, where the morning stars are represented as singing together, and the sons of God as shouting for joy, over the creation of our earth (Job xxxviii. 7).

"And lastly, the same expression is found in the Book of Daniel; but in the singular number, and with the necessary difference that *bar* is the word used for son instead of *ben*, the singular of the latter being unknown in Chaldee. Nebuchadnezzar exclaims that he sees four men walking in the midst of the fire, and that the form of the fourth is like a son of God, by which he evidently means a supernatural or angelic being, distinct as such from others.

"It thus appears that the sons of God are angelic beings: and the mysterious statement respecting them in the sixth chapter of Genesis seems to refer to a second and deeper apostasy on the part of some of the High Ones on high. But these more daring rebels are not found among the spirits of darkness which now haunt the air. They no longer retain their position as principalities and powers of the world, or even their liberty; but may be identified with the imprisoned criminals of whom Peter tells us that, after they had sinned, God spared them not, 'but cast them down to Hell, and delivered them into chains of darkness, to be reserved unto judgment' (2 Pet. ii. 4). Jude also mentions their present condition in similar terms (Jude 6), and the context of either passage indicates with sufficient clearness the nature of their sin."

Such is Mr. Pember's presentation of the theory, given practically in full length. We turn now to Dr. Bullinger's *How to Enjoy the Bible*, for a rather shorter quotation.

"The great promise and prophecy had gone forth in Genesis iii. 15, that 'the seed of the woman' should come into the world, and should finally crush the head of the Old Serpent. Satan's object therefore was to frustrate this counsel of God.

"Having as yet no clue as to the line by which 'the seed of the woman' should come into the world, his first effort was to corrupt and destroy the whole human race. This he carried out as described in Genesis vi. and Jude 6. 'The sons of

God' were angels; 'the angels who sinned.' All beings who
are the direct creation of God are called his 'sons.' Adam
was 'a son of God' (Gen. v. 1; Luke iii. 38). We are not.
By nature we are the sons of Adam begotten in his likeness
(Gen. v. 3). The New nature in us makes us 'sons of God,'
because that is God's own new-creation work (Eph. ii. 10;
2 Cor. v. 17; Rom. viii. 14–17). For the same reason also,
angels are called 'sons of God,' because they are the direct
creation of God. In the Old Testament the expression
always has this meaning. Before Adam was created 'the
morning stars sang together, and all the sons of God shouted
for joy' (Job xxxviii. 7). An angel was sent to the lions'
den to shut the lions' mouths (Dan. vi. 22), as another was
sent to the fiery furnace to deliver Jehovah's servants; this
angel is called 'a son of God' (for there is no article).

"They cannot (in Gen. vi) be the seed of Seth, as is generally
taught, because they are contrasted with 'the daughters of
MEN'; which shows they must be of a different nature.

"We know from Genesis vi how nearly that great plot succeeded; how the whole earth was corrupted (Gen. vi. 11, 12).
All except Noah's family were tainted with this uncanny
and unholy breed called '*Nephilim.*' Noah was *tamim*, i.e.,
'without blemish,' as the word for 'perfect' here is generally
rendered elsewhere. All had to be destroyed by the Flood;
but the angels who sinned are 'reserved' in 'chains' and 'in
prison' (1 Pet. iii. 19; 2 Pet. ii. 4; Jude 6), for their judgment at a yet future day."

Perhaps we ought in fairness just to add the following brief
quotation from Dr. Bullinger's well-known *Companion Bible*,
so that we have his case completely.

"That there was a fall of angels is certain from Jude 6. The
nature of their fall is clearly stated in the same verse. They
left their own *oiketerion*. This word occurs only in 2 Cor.
v. 2 and Jude 6, where it is used of the spiritual (or resurrection) body.

"The nature of their sin is stated to be 'in like manner' to
that of the subsequent sins of Sodom and Gomorrha,

Jude 7. The time of their fall is given as having taken place 'in the days of Noah' (1 Pet. iii. 20; 2 Pet. ii. 5), though there may have been a prior fall which caused the end of 'the world that then was' (Gen. i. 1, 2; 2 Pet. iii. 6). For this sin they are 'reserved unto judgment' (2 Pet. ii. 4), and are 'in prison' (1 Pet. iii. 19).

"Their progeny, called *Nephilim* (translated 'giants'), were monsters of iniquity, and being superhuman in size and character, had to be destroyed. This was the one and only object of the Flood."

Such, then, is the theory that the "sons of God" in Genesis vi were "the angels that sinned." The two authors whom we have quoted are able exponents of it; and the quotations which we have given do full justice to them both. Moreover, we ourselves would be the first to acknowledge that there is a certain lucidity of argument and a felicity of reference to seemingly corroborative passages of Scripture which give the theory a ready appeal.

Yet can we really accept it, however plausible it may seem as it flows from the pens of Pember and Bullinger? We ourselves would submit that we *cannot*. We believe that a more careful reflection and examination decidedly disqualify it, as we shall now try to show. There are certain difficulties involved in it which, to our own judgment at least, seem quite insuperable. There are physiological and psychological problems raised by this theory, which its advocates gratuitously ignore, which nevertheless at once show it to be pretty well absurd. And, further, some of the supposedly ancillary passages of Scripture to which the advocates of the theory refer, when more closely considered, scarcely give even doubtful support to it.

THE PSYCHO-PHYSIOLOGICAL DIFFICULTY

First, then, let us briefly consider the *psycho-physiological* difficulty involved in this theory that the "sons of God" in Genesis vi were angels. Surely, if we think penetratively at all on this subject, we must soon see that any such cohabiting of angels with human womenkind as this theory supposes is unthinkable.

Let us be frank and explicit. The angels are bodiless, purely spiritual beings, and sexless. Being bodiless and sexless means that they are without sex organs, and that they are therefore absolutely incapable of sensuous experiences or sexual processes; nor are they capable of procreation or reproduction in any way whatever. There is no need to refer to this or that or the other text: the whole teaching of the Bible concerning the angels stands solidly behind that affirmation.

As for the suggestion that these evil angels somehow took human bodies to themselves and thus became capable of sex functions, it is sheer absurdity, as anyone can see. Both on psychological and physiological grounds it is unthinkable. We all know what an exquisitely delicate, intricate, intimate, sensitive inter-relation and inter-reaction there exists between the human body and the human mind or soul. This is because soul and body came into being together through the wonderful process of a human *birth*, and are mysteriously *united in one human personality*. Thus, and only thus, is it that the sensations of the body become experiences of the mind. This psycho-physical parallelism of the human personality is a mystery; but it is an absolute and universal reality.

Now if angels merely took bodies and miraculously indwelt them for the time being, their doing so could not have made them in the slightest degree able to experience the sensations of those bodies, even if those bodies themselves could have been capable of real sensations, which is greatly doubtful; for the angels and those temporarily occupied bodies, not having come into being together by a real human birth as one personality, there could not be any such inter-reaction as that which exists in the case of the *human* mind and body. Indeed, the bodies could not have been real bodies of flesh and blood at all, when we come to think of it; for without being inhabited by the human spirit, the human flesh-and-blood body dies. Bodies *occupied* by angels simply could not be normal human bodies of flesh and blood.

Perhaps we can best bring this home to our minds by that most wonderful of all illustrations, the incarnation of our divine Lord Himself. Our Lord's incarnation was no mere occupation of a human body. Ponder this a moment. Look back over the

Old Testament. We find there a notable succession of instances in which the pre-incarnate Christ communicated in bodily form with men. These are known theologically as the *Theophanies.* In Genesis xviii, One of the "three men" who visited Abraham is singled out and addressed as "my Lord." This One speaks as being indeed divine, promising the birth of Isaac, and is actually called "Jehovah" (verses 17, 20, 22, 26, 33). It is with Him that Abraham intercedes for Sodom, and by Him that retribution is afterward inflicted on that wicked city. Again and again there are the appearances of One who bears the title, "the Angel of Jehovah," but who speaks and acts as being actually *one* with God. As such did He appear to Hagar (Gen. xvi); and similarly to Jacob, as, "I am the God of Bethel," and later as the Man who wrestled with Jacob until daybreak at Jabbok, of whom Jacob says, "I have seen God face to face" (Gen. xxxii. 30); similarly to Moses in the burning bush of Horeb, as "I am the God of thy father Abraham . . ."; and so to Gideon, as "Jehovah is with thee"; and so to Samson's parents; and so to others. The data are such as to indicate that this "Angel of Jehovah" was none other than the pre-incarnate Son of God, revealing Himself in bodily form from time to time. Besides serving their immediate purpose, these appearances were a means of preparing men's minds for the coming miracle of the *Incarnation* by which the Son of God should actually become one with the human race as the Son of Man.

But let us be once and for all clear about this, that those Old Testament "theophanies" of the Son of God in bodily form were not any such thing as real *incarnation.* In those "theophanies" He merely utilized some visible, bodily form which was prepared for the purpose of the moment and discarded afterward. But when, at Bethlehem, Christ entered our human life by way of a real human birth of a human mother, he was doing something far more than merely occupying a human form: for in that supreme miracle of history He was verily taking to Himself our human *nature*; He was verily *becoming human* to remain so for ever, though, of course, at the same time necessarily remaining truly God.

Now apply this to the theory that those "sons of God" in Genesis vi were angels. We say again that when our Lord Jesus came into this world to be our Saviour, He did not merely take to Himself a human body and inhabit it. That would not have made Him human. It would only have been another "theophany." He took to Himself our human *nature* itself; and (mark well) to do this *it was absolutely necessary that He should be born into our life and nature by a human birth of a human mother.* If, then, those "sons of God" in Genesis vi were angels, the only way they could have become human and have married and have had children (as verses 1 and 4 say) is by their having undergone a real human *birth*—that is, by their having been incarnated and born of human mothers, but without human fathers!

There is no escape from this necessity, if we accept the Pember and Bullinger theory. Therefore, on this ground alone, we simply *cannot* accept their theory; for the idea that such an incarnation of angels took place, by their being born of human mothers, without human fathers, and by the hundred or thousand (which, remember, we should have to suppose) is preposterous.

Quite apart from other considerations, such a theory surely casts a libel on the character of God Himself. We simply cannot believe that God would allow such a wholesale angel-incarnation, and then inflict judgment for it upon the *human* race— for the judgment of the Flood is definitely said to be for *human* sin (see verses 3, 5, 6). If it be said that the evil angels committed this monstrosity *in defiance* of God, and *without* His permission, we reply that in this case the thing *could not happen* without the divine permission, for it involves *creative* power, which not even the angels possess, but God only.

What, then, do Mr. Pember and Dr. Bullinger say to this? Dr. Bullinger conveniently says nothing at all. Mr. Pember uneasily tries to dismiss it by simply saying, " Those who advance it (i.e., the above objection) lay claim to a more intimate acquaintance with angelic nature than we can concede as possible." We cannot keep back a smile at Mr. Pember's words, for, of course, it is he himself, in his theory of angel cross-breeding with human beings, who assumes the "more intimate acquaintance with angelic nature" than can be conceded! So there we are; they really have no reply. In our own judgment, this one psycho-physiological objection alone is enough to discredit their theory.

OTHER DIFFICULTIES OF THE ANGEL THEORY

But besides what we have called the psycho-physiological difficulty, there are other considerations which, taken together, seem to militate conclusively against the "angel" theory. Perhaps the best way to deal with these is just to run the eye again through the Pember and Bullinger quotations already given, and deal with the points in question just as they successively occur.

The Wording of Genesis vi. *1, 2*.

Mr. Pember says: "When *men*, we are told, began to multiply on the face of the earth, and daughters were born unto them, the sons of God saw the daughters of *men*. Now by 'men' in each case the whole human race is evidently signified, the descendants of Cain and Seth alike. Hence the 'sons of God' are plainly distinguished from the generation of Adam." Bullinger says the same thing.

Yet is this really any argument at all? There are two factors which completely "knock the bottom out of it." First, if it was these evil *angels* who were sinning so grievously in thus taking them wives of all which they chose, why does the very next sentence say, "And the Lord said: My Spirit shall not always strive with *MAN*"? On the Pember-Bullinger hypothesis the striving of the Spirit should have been with the evil angels, not men! Just fancy, the Spirit striving with *men* for the sinning of *angels*! No, that bit of exegesis will not do! More about it later.

But second, in those words, "The sons of God saw the daughters of men that they were fair, and took them wives of all which they chose," the emphasis is not on the word "men," as Pember and Bullinger aver, but upon the last clause—"wives *of all which they chose*." The very position of this clause at the end of the sentence gives it the emphasis. And the emphasis, of course, is that wives were now being chosen, not only in defiant disregard of the will of God, but in the plural, that is, polygamously. With the disregard of the will of God came the practice of having more wives than one; and with this there increasingly developed the corruption of which the chapter speaks. No, we cannot allow Pember and Bullinger to have it that the emphasis is on "men" as in contrast with the "sons of God." Their exegesis on this point, we believe, is again at fault.

The Title, "Sons of God."

The keystone in the Pember-Bullinger arch is that the title, "sons of God," *must* refer to angels, in Genesis vi, because this title is used only of angels elsewhere in the Old Testament. Pember says: "The expression, 'sons of God,' occurs but four times in other parts of the Old Testament, and is in each of these cases indisputably used of angelic beings." Bullinger speaks to the same effect. And they both tell us that the *reason* why this title is reserved for angels, in the Old Testament, is that it is only used of beings who are "directly created by the Divine hand, and not born of other beings of their own order."

What shall we say to this? Well, to begin with, the very fact that the expression occurs *only* four times in the Old Testament outside of Genesis vi should have made the exponents of the "angel" theory wary against drawing startling conclusions from slender data, especially so inasmuch as three out of the four are all in one book (Job i. 6, ii. 1, xxxviii. 7), and the other one (Dan. iii. 25) is not the same expression in the original. In fact we may claim this Daniel text right away as *against* the theory, for the following reason: When Nebuchadnezzar looked into that "burning, fiery furnace," he exclaimed, "Lo, I see four men, loose, and walking in the midst of the fire . . . and the form of the fourth is like a (not 'the') son of God!" Now if, as Pember and Bullinger say, the Old Testament expression, "sons of God," refers only to angels, then Nebuchadnezzar should have seen in that furnace three men and one *angel*; but no, he saw "four *men*"! Whatever peculiarity may have distinguished that fourth figure, the form was *human*: there is no getting over that.

What now about the texts in Job? We believe that in these texts the expression, "sons of God," probably *does* refer to angels: yet strange as it may seem, the very fact that angels *are* called "sons of God" in these Job verses convinces us that the same title in Genesis vi *cannot* mean angels. We will give our reasons for this.

Both in Job i. 6 and ii. 1, we have the same words—"There was a day when the sons of God came to present themselves before Jehovah; and Satan came also among them." Mark, then, the sharp distinction here made between these angels and Satan. Why should the distinction be made?—for Satan himself is a mighty angel, or spirit-being, and therefore, strictly speaking, according to the Pember and Bullinger theory, Satan himself is a "son of God," for (in Mr. Pember's words) he is a being "directly created by the Divine hand." Yet to call Satan a "son of God" is now preposterous. That these "sons of God" in Job i. 6 and ii. 1 are *unfallen* angels seems clear from the sharp difference made between them and Satan; and it seems to be made the more certain by the further reference in Job xxxviii. 7, where we read of these unfallen sons of God "shouting for joy" over the creative work of God. We may settle it in our minds, then, that the title, "sons of God" would never be used anywhere of *evil* angels. But if so, what about Genesis vi? According to Pember and Bullinger, those "sons of God" were *evil* angels, who committed that further and most monstrous outrage. But how could such *evil* angels be called "sons of God"? That is another problem of the angel theory.

It is worthy of note, also, that although we ourselves have agreed that the title, "sons of God," in Job refers to angels, there are those who do not. We were quite surprised recently to find how cogently it may be argued that those "sons of God" who came "to present themselves before Jehovah," were not angels at all, but "the godly men of the time who came for worship in the presence of the Lord," and that they presented themselves before a real, visible presence of the Lord such as we find again and again in the Old Testament *Theophanies*. We cannot here go into all the *pros* and *cons* of this interpretation; but it is well worth bearing in mind; and, of course, if it be a true interpretation then it demolishes at once the Pember-Bullinger bulwark that the title, "sons of God," in the Old Testament, is only used of angels. (See Appendix on this matter, where we give a quotation of considerable significance from Mr. George Rapkin's book on Genesis. Some of the arguments in favour of this interpretation certainly seem singularly cogent.)

The Nephilim.

But now there crops up another contradiction of the angel theory which again puts its champions on the horns of a dilemma. Genesis vi. 4 says: "There were giants in the earth in those days; and also, after that, when the sons of God came in unto the daughters of men, and they bare children to them, the same became mighty men which were of old, men of renown."

The Hebrew word here translated as "giants" is *Nephilim*. Mr. Pember has it that these *Nephilim* were the fallen angels, alias the so-called "sons of God." Dr. Bullinger has it that they were rather the *progeny* resulting from the coition of the sinning angels with the women of earth. He says: "Their (i.e., the angels') progeny, called *Nephilim*, were monsters of iniquity; and, being superhuman in size and character, had to be destroyed. This was the one and only object of the Flood."

Yet a simple reference to Genesis vi. 4 will show Bullinger's blunder here. It says: "The *Nephilim* were in the earth in those days: and, also, AFTER THAT, when the sons of God came in unto the daughters of men, and they bare children to them, the same became mighty men." So, whoever these *Nephilim* were, they certainly were already on earth before ever the offspring of the supposed angel-human unions came into being: the words, "*after that*," in the verse, make this most definite. The offspring of those unions between the "sons of God" and the daughters of men are called "mighty men" and "men of renown," but not *Nephilim*. (More about this later.)

However, both these two writers, assuming that the *Nephilim* were the sinning angels and their progeny, tell us that the Flood came to destroy this unholy brood. But if that is so, what about the Book of Numbers, chapter xiii. 33, where we read of the *Nephilim* as still being a race of people, over eight hundred years after the Flood? Ten of the twelve spies who reconnoitred Canaan came back saying, "And there we saw the *Nephilim*, sons of Anak of the *Nephilim*; and we were in our own sight as grasshoppers." This is a very awkward jolt for the Pember-Bullinger scheme. What can they say? Well, they are both obliged to argue that there must have been a *still further* occurrence of angels leaving "their first estate" and invading the

earth to marry human wives, sometime *after* the Flood! Yet
there is not a speck of suggestion anywhere in Scripture of any
such thing! And it would mean that God had allowed the unholy
traffic to go on again for hundreds of years! See the covert way
in which Pember puts it—"A similar occurrence *after* the Deluge
agrees with the passage in Numbers where the sons of Anak
are said to have been *Nephilim*, and seems also to account for
God's command that the whole race of the Canaanites should
be extirpated." But on this theory it is the sinning *angels* which
should have been "extirpated," not the deceived and helpless
human victims! Surely, the real reason why these Canaanites
were to be destroyed was *their own* vileness (see Lev. xviii. 24,
25, and xx. 23).

But now see what the ingenious Dr. Bullinger writes about
it: "We read of the *Nephilim* again in Numbers xiii. 33. . . .
How, it may be asked, could this be, if they were all destroyed
in the Flood? The answer is contained in Genesis vi. 4, where
we read: 'There were *Nephilim* in the earth in those days (i.e.,
in the days of Noah); and also AFTER THAT, when the sons
of God came in unto the daughters of men, and they bare children
to them, the same became (the) mighty men (Heb. *gibbor*, the
heroes) which were of old, men of renown'. . . . So that 'after
that,' i.e., after the Flood, there was a second irruption of these
fallen angels, evidently smaller in number and more limited in
area, for they were for the most part confined to Canaan, and
were in fact known as 'the nations of Canaan'."

That is enough to make any reader gasp, "What next!?"
We are asked to believe that the words, "after that," suddenly
switch the remainder of the verse to a point hundreds of years
after the Flood, so that these "mighty men" and "men of
renown" which were "*of old*" did not belong to Noah's days at
all, but to a later age! Remember, *Moses* wrote the first five
books of our Bible; and he wrote very near the time that the
ten spies brought back their report (Num. xiii. 33) concerning
the presence of the *Nephilim* in Canaan. If, then, in Genesis
vi. 4, Moses meant the words, "after that," to switch us suddenly
over from the pre-Flood era to an irruption of angels hundreds
of years later, and to their prodigy-offspring (*Nephilim*) who
were alive in his own time, he would surely not have said, "the

same became mighty men which were *OF OLD*, men of renown"!
He would have said, "the same are the mighty men of renown
to-day."

Bullinger's treatment of Genesis vi. 4 is thoroughly unworthy.
The verse simply enough tells us that the offspring of the "sons
of God" and the "daughters of men" became mighty men of
renown; but Bullinger first makes the *Nephilim* the offspring
of the "sons of God" and the daughters of men; then he makes
the "sons of God" in this verse to be a still further irruption
of immoral angels centuries later; and then makes the "mighty
men of renown" into a *new* breed of *Nephilim* still living in the
time of Moses! It is wonderful how well-meaning men can distort
Scripture to fit a theory!

THE SUPPOSED NEW TESTAMENT CONFIRMATION

Another very strong point, if not the strongest, with **Mr.**
Pember and **Dr. Bullinger**, is that their theory is proved, or **at**
least strongly corroborated, by the New Testament. The three
texts which supposedly certify it are 1 Peter iii. 19, 20; **2 Peter**
ii. 4; and Jude 6. Take Dr. Bullinger's words again:

"That there was a fall of angels is certain from Jude 6. The
nature of their fall is clearly stated in the same verse. They
left their own *oiketerion*. This word occurs only in 2 Corinthians v. 2 and Jude 6, where it is used of the spiritual (or
resurrection) body. The nature of their sin is stated to be
'in like manner' to that of the subsequent sins of Sodom
and Gomorrha (Jude 7). The time of their fall is given as
having taken place 'in the days of Noah' (1 Pet. iii. 20;
2 Pet. ii. 5). . . . . For this sin they are 'reserved unto judgment' (2 Pet. ii. 4), and are 'in prison' (1 Pet. iii. 19)."

Dr. Bullinger goes further, and says, in his *How to Enjoy the*
Bible (p. 190), that Christ went in His resurrection body **and**
preached to these fallen angels in the Hades abyss:

"He had a glorious triumph as well. He went in His resurrection body and made proclamation of it to 'the-in-prison-
spirits.' What and who can these be? To answer this ques-

tion we have to go a little further afield, but not far. The same Peter tells us overleaf, in 2 Peter ii. 4, of the angels that sinned in the days of Noah, and who are now cast down to Tartarus and there 'delivered into chains of darkness to be reserved unto judgment'."

Now one of the difficulties in replying concisely to a reasoner like Dr. Bullinger is that when once he gets borne along by a theory he often jumps so blithely from one gratuitous assumption to another that it takes you all your time correcting him on this and that and the other point in the process, before ever you come to show the fallacy of his main contention.

This is so in the foregoing quotation. He simply takes for granted point after point which we ourselves not only contradict, but with little difficulty will disprove. Just note some of these:

(1) He *assumes* that these "spirits in prison" are angels: but that is something which needs to be proved.

(2) He *assumes* that these "spirits in prison" in 1 Peter iii. 19 are the same as the angels in 2 Peter ii. 4 and Jude 6 (and, of course, that both are identical with those "sons of God" in Genesis vi). But this also needs to be proved!

(3) He asserts that 1 Peter iii. 20 and 2 Peter ii. 5 give "the time of their fall" as "in the days of Noah"; which in one case is right and in the other wrong.

(4) He asserts that Jude 7 declares their sin to be "in like manner" to that of Sodom and Gomorrha; which is at least very questionable.

Let us look, then, briefly at these three places in the New Testament which Pember and Bullinger claim for their theory. We turn first to 1 Peter iii. 18–20. We give the rendering of the English Revised Version:

"Christ also suffered for sins once, the righteous for the unrighteous, that he might bring us to God; being put to death in the flesh, but quickened in the spirit; in which also he went and preached unto the spirits in prison, which aforetime were disobedient, when the longsuffering of God waited in the days of Noah . . ."

F

Now admittedly these verses contain some rather puzzling references, but fortunately we need not go into all of these before we can settle it conclusively that these "spirits in prison" were *not* the "angels that sinned," as Bullinger and his co-theorists allege. We agree, of course, that Peter's words connect these "spirits in prison" with Noah's day, and we agree that the "prison" here is Hades. Yet for all that, these "spirits in prison" simply cannot be "the angels that sinned" (2 Pet. ii. 4) and who "left their first estate" (Jude 6), or angels at all, for a reason which we will now submit.

Dr. Bullinger has fallen into a fault for which his writings often blame others—that is inadequate attention to the context. Let us see. To quote Peter literally from the Greek, our Lord, "having been put to death in flesh, but quickened in spirit," went and "to the in-prison-spirits preached." What did He preach? Well, Peter's word here for "preach" is *kerusso*, a very common New Testament word for preaching the Gospel (used between forty and fifty times of our Lord's preaching and the Apostles' preaching of the Gospel). And *who*, then, were these "spirits" in Hades, to whom our Lord preached? Well, only a few verses later, in chapter iv. 6, which continues the same subject irrespective of the chapter break, Peter tells us *what* was preached, *why* it was preached, and *who* these "spirits" were. He says: "For this cause was the *Gospel* preached also to them that are dead, that they might be judged according to *MEN* in the flesh, but live to God in the spirit." So then, whatever other problems there may be about this verse, it leaves simply no doubt that these "spirits" who beforetime were "disobedient in the days of Noah" were *MEN*, not angels!

But see now how Bullinger, having *assumed* that these "spirits in prison" are fallen angels, must start inventing ideas and then distorting the Scripture to make it fit. He himself realizes that our Lord could not very well be thought of as having gone to preach the "Gospel" to fallen *angels*, for the Gospel of the Son of God who became *human* in order to save the race of *Adam* is obviously for fallen *men*; so he is at pains to argue that our Lord's preaching to these supposed fallen angels was *not* the Gospel, but a proclamation of our Lord's resurrection-triumph, "to show them that all this triumph was in spite of the Satanic plot referred to in Genesis vi, and in which they had so great a share and so great a guilt." Now could there be a more artificial or theatrical "explanation" than that?

Dr. Bullinger's invention, however, only lands him in further trouble; for having said that our Lord went to these "spirits in prison" simply to proclaim His resurrection-triumph, he has to make our Lord's visit to Hades occur *after His resurrection*, whereas the only such visit that Scripture knows was *between* His death and resurrection (Acts ii. 31; Eph. iv. 9, 10). Surely, in I Peter iii. 19, Peter is echoing and amplifying his own words in Acts ii. 31, concerning our Lord's going into Hades between His death and His resurrection. Why, the very wording of I Peter iii. 19 shows this: "Being put to death in flesh, but quickened *in spirit*; in which also (i.e., in *spirit*, not in flesh) he went and preached unto the spirits in prison." Not only the wording, but the parallel here makes the meaning as clear as can be—our Lord, being no longer in the flesh, but in the spirit, went and preached to these who themselves were no longer in the flesh but in the spirit. Where does Dr. Bullinger find the slightest warrant in Scripture for our Lord's going *again* into Hades, this time with His glorified *body*? The well-meaning old doctor is no longer on earth to say; but perhaps some of his followers could tell us.

Nor is even that the end of Dr. Bullinger's gymnastics here; for having so mis-explained Peter's words in chapter iii. 18–20, he is simply obliged to do likewise with that later verse which is so awkward for him, that is, chapter iv. 6, which says, "For this cause was the Gospel preached also to them that are dead, that they might be judged according to men in the flesh, but live according to God in the spirit." What unbiased mind can read these words without seeing at once their connection with those earlier words in the same context, about the "spirits in prison"? But Dr. Bullinger, having made those human spirits into *angels*, cannot have it that the Gospel was preached to *them*, so he now makes chapter iv. 6 to mean that the Gospel was preached to men and women of former times who are *now* dead, but who had the Gospel preached to them in advance, *before* they died! Really, when one starts tracking down the fallacy of a Bullinger theory, one has to follow him—

O'er moor and fen,
O'er crag and torrent,
   Till the night is gone!

We ourselves have often found rich reward in Dr. Bullinger's painstaking researches in the Bible, and would be the first to acknowledge indebtedness; but for all that, some of his text-manipulations leave us exclaiming, "What artful making-things-fit even the best-intentioned expositors can get up to, if they are not careful, in order to bolster up a theory!"

So far as 1 Peter iii. 18–20 is concerned, we must leave Dr. Bullinger. One thing we have at any rate made clear: those "spirits in prison" were definitely not "the angels that sinned," but *HUMAN* spirits.

2 *Peter ii. 4, and Jude* 6.

The remaining two texts (2 Pet. ii. 4 and Jude 6) can be dealt with quite briefly. Dr. Bullinger says that 2 Peter ii. 4 gives "the time of their (i.e., the angels') fall as having taken place 'in the days of Noah'." But if we read the text with its context, we find that it actually *separates* the fall of the angels from Noah's time. Peter gives us *three* examples of divine judgment on the wicked—first, "the angels that sinned" (verse 4), second, the pre-Flood era (verse 5), third, Sodom and Gomorrha (verse 6). Here they are:

(1) "For if God spared not the angels that sinned, but cast them down to hell, and delivered them into chains of darkness, to be reserved unto judgment;

(2) "And spared not the old world, but saved Noah the eighth person, a preacher of righteousness, bringing in the flood upon the world of the ungodly;

(3) "And turning the cities of Sodom and Gomorrha into ashes, condemned them with an overthrow, making them an example unto those that after should live ungodly . . ."

Now if, as the angel-theory advocates say, number 1 happened at the same time as number 2, why not 2 at the same time as 3? Is it not the more reasonable thing to see that Peter here speaks in correct order, of three events which occurred successively, and not simultaneously? It is; and that means, of course, that this fall of angels happened *before* Noah's time.

Take, now, the last of the three New Testament texts, that is, Jude 6. It is claimed that this verse reveals the *nature* of the sin into which the angels fell, because it says (so it is claimed) they "left their own habitation" and sinned *"in like manner"* to the people of Sodom and Gomorrha. But does the verse really teach that the angels sinned in that sexual way? Let us see. Here are the two verses concerned:

"And the angels which kept not their first estate, but left their own habitation. He hath reserved in everlasting chains under darkness unto the judgment of the great day. Even as Sodom and Gomorrha, and the cities about them in like manner, giving themselves over to fornication, and going after strange flesh, are set forth for an example, suffering the vengeance of eternal fire" (Jude 6, 7).

Those who teach that the "sons of God" in Genesis vi were these angels of Jude 6 make much of the words, *"in like manner,"* here in Jude 7. Yet instead of meaning that the people of Sodom and Gomorrha *sinned* "in like manner" to those wicked angels, do not the words mean that they are a *WARNING EXAMPLE* "in like manner" as the angels? Read the verse again, with that emphasis:

"Even as Sodom and Gomorrha and the cities about them, *IN LIKE MANNER,* having given themselves over to fornication and having gone after strange flesh, *ARE SET FORTH AS AN EXAMPLE,* suffering the vengeance of eternal fire."

But if *that* reading of the text be grammatically unacceptable, there is much to be said for the punctuation given in the Authorized Version:

"Even as Sodom and Gomorrha, *AND THE CITIES ABOUT THEM IN LIKE MANNER,* having given themselves over. . . ."

This joins the "in like manner" to the cities of the plain instead of to the angels. We have noted the objection of Alford and a few others to this, but in our own judgment it is feeble.

However, even if we agreed that the words, "in like manner," connected the *sinning* of Sodom and Gomorrha with that of the angels—even then it certainly need mean no more than that their sin was *fundamentally* similar (i.e., rebellion and apostasy) and not identical in detail.

And there is a further fact which is most conclusive of all, on grammatical grounds, against making this text teach that the angels sinned in the same way as the people of Sodom and Gomorrha. It is this: Even if we agreed that the words, "in like manner," described the nature of the *sinning*—even then the fact remains that this text simply DOES NOT SAY that the angels sinned in like manner to the people of Sodom and Gomorrha. It puts it the other way round, and says that it was the people of Sodom and Gomorrha who sinned "in like manner" *to the angels*! No strict exegesis can ignore this. See what it means. If the angels' sin *had* been sexual, it would have been quite enough for Jude to leave it that the people of Sodom and Gomorrha sinned "in like manner," without needing to specify again that it was sexual. Yet as soon as he has said that the people of Sodom and Gomorrha sinned "in like manner" to the angels, he adds, "giving themselves over to fornication, and going after strange flesh." Surely the very necessity to add these words indicates the point at which the sin of Sodom and Gomorrha *diverged* from that of the angels!

This is made the more certain by Jude's use of that adjective *heteras*, which the Authorized Version translates as "strange," but which simply means "other." As Keil remarks, the fact that they went after "*other* flesh" means that they had flesh of their own, which the angels *have not*!

And still more devastating to the Pember-Bullinger interpretation is the fact that if Jude *had* meant us to understand that these angels sinned in precisely the same way as the Sodomites, then these angels *could not* have been those "sons of God" in Genesis vi; for the sin in Genesis vi is not the wholesale fornication and beastly homo-sexual vileness which the Scriptures always connect with Sodom, but unhallowed (and probably polygamous) *marriage* unions. There is absolutely no hint in Genesis vi that those "sons of God" sinned Sodomishly.

Nor is even this all against the Pember-Bullinger usage of Jude 6. The text says that the sinning angels "left their own habitation." The Greek word here given as "habitation" is *oiketerion*, and, as Bullinger points out, this word occurs only once elsewhere in the New Testament, that is, in 2 Corinthians v. 2, where it is used to denote the believer's resurrection body, or "spirit-body" as Bullinger has called it. On this basis, then, it is supposed that the angels left their spirit-bodies to cohabit with women on earth. But who says the angels *have* bodies? Is not the whole teaching of Scripture that they are pure spirit, as to their substance, and therefore bodiless? And even if the sinning angels *had* "spirit-bodies," in that immaterial state, being absolutely without any nervous system or senses such as we have in the human body, how could they possibly have felt attraction for something fleshly to which they were incapable of response? And yet again, if those angels left "spirit-bodies," where did they leave them? And where are they now? Such bodies are not subject to decomposition! They cannot be buried! And how did the angels become human?—for they simply could not become husbands and rear children apart from actual incarnation as human beings. What the Pember-Bullinger theory really asks us to accept is that these angels actually un-angeled and then humanized themselves!

Bullinger, moreover, would never have founded such an argument on a comparison of Jude 6 with 2 Corinthians v. 2, if he had noted something which he has quite overlooked. That is, in 2 Corinthians v. 2, the word *oiketerion* is used of the resurrection body which will belong to each believer *individually*; whereas in Jude 6, the one *oiketerion* covers the angels *collectively*. They "left their own (plural) habitation (singular)." The word in Jude 6 has no reference to individual angel-bodies: it denotes rather an exalted *plane* of being, as does also the preceding clause of the text—"the angels which kept not their own *principality*" (see E. R. V.).

So much, then, for the three New Testament texts which are supposed to substantiate the Pember-Bullinger theory. Three things are very clear:

(1) In 1 Peter iii. 18–20, it is *not angels at all* which are spoken of but the departed spirits of human beings;

(2) In 2 Peter ii. 4, the *time* when the fall of "the angels that sinned" took place is *not* said to be the time of Genesis vi;

(3) In Jude 6, the evil angels are *not* identified with the "sons of God" in Genesis vi, nor is the sin of these angels said to be the same, in any close correspondence, with the sins of Sodom and Gomorrha.

That is our finding, after careful examination; and it means, of course, that there is no New Testament warrant whatever for the theory that the "sons of God" in Genesis vi were angels.

WHERE DID THE ANGEL THEORY COME FROM?

Perhaps, then, we may be asked: If this "angel" theory may be so completely disposed of, how did it originate and come to have such vogue?

We must go back to a couple of centuries B.C. From about 200 B.C. to the later part of the first century A.D., there appeared from time to time certain pseudepigraphic, apocalyptic writings, the earlier of which, it would seem, emanated from a Jewish sect known as the Essenes. They are called "apocalyptic" because they affect to be visionary unveilings of the future; and they are called "pseudepigraphic" because they were written under falsely assumed names, and purport to have come from earlier times than that in which they were actually written. Such spurious writings could not hope to survive the test of time and investigation, yet it is easy to appreciate that for a time they would have a rather exciting and considerable influence.

One of these is the Book of Enoch (which, however, is really several in one); and it is here, in this Book of Enoch, written (at least the part of it with which we are concerned) probably soon after 200 B.C., that we first find this idea of the sinning angels associated with Genesis vi; and probably the pseudonymous author got his idea from pagan mythologies with their crude stories of gods coming down to earth and indulging sensual appetites. The book is quite plentiful in errors and far-fetched extravagances. It says that the number of angels who committed the outrage of Genesis vi was two hundred. The fanciful angelology of these apocalyptic pseudepigraphs is one of their conspicuous features; and this is pre-eminently so with the Book of Enoch.

Now this Book of Enoch seems to have had a quite considerable popular appeal for some time, two instances of which here concern us. The first is in connection with the famous Septuagint Version of the Hebrew Scriptures into Greek. In the third century B.C., when Hebrew was less and less spoken among the Jews, and Greek was more and more the international language, a translation of the Hebrew Scriptures into Greek became an urgent necessity. Such a translation was made, at Alexandria, under royal patronage (so we are told), and is known to us as the "Septuagint" (from *Septuaginta*, the Latin for seventy) because of the tradition that it was made by seventy Jewish scribes. This Septuagint Version quickly became the standard "Bible" of the Jews. Later it was the accepted version of the Old Testament among Christians. The writers of our New Testament repeatedly give their Old Testament quotations from it. And it lies very largely behind our English version of the Old Testament.

Well now, the original manuscripts of the Septuagint are lost to us; and it is one of the fascinating functions of textual criticism to collate the various manuscript *copies* of it which have come down to us. Of these, the three oldest and most important are (1) the Codex Sinaiticus, written in the fourth century A.D., (2) the Codex Alexandrinus, written in the fifth century, (3) the Codex Vaticanus, written in the fourth century. Now the second of these, gives the word "angels" in Genesis vi. 2, instead of "sons of God" (and, of course, advocates of the "angel" theory of Genesis vi. 2 have made much of this). But can we accept the Codex Alexandrinus in that particular verse? The answer is, NO, for the following reasons:

(1) Not one of the *Hebrew* manuscripts has "angels" in that verse. They all have "sons of God."

(2) The other leading *Greek* manuscripts have "sons of God" in that verse.

(3) The Codex Alexandrinus is *not* a copy of the *original* manuscript of the Septuagint, but only of one of the many *copies*

which were made in the last two centuries of the B.C. era
and the opening centuries of the A.D. era: and we know that
textual corruptions had set in by then (see article in *International Standard Bible Encyclopaedia*).

(4) The obvious probability is that the word "angel" was inserted
by a transcriber holding the fascinating new idea of Genesis
vi. 1–4 which had been popularized by the Book of Enoch.

So much for the Pentateuch; but it is also to be noted that
the Jewish historian, Josephus (born 37 B.C.), evidently accepted
the "angel" idea, as we see from a brief reference to Genesis vi,
in his "Antiquities of the Jews." That, however, is not surprising, as Josephus himself tells us that he had earlier been
connected with the Essenes, the Jewish sect from which the
pseudepigraph Enoch presumably emanated.

Such, then, is the order—first in the Book of Enoch, then
slipping into transcriptions of the Septuagint, and made further
public through the pen of Josephus. From that point it was
easy to connect up the idea with such verses as 2 Peter ii. 4
and Jude 6. Thus we find some of the early Christian Fathers
adopting it, though after fuller discussion it seems to have been
the later consensus of the early church that the opinion was
untenable.

The fact is, that if we keep strictly faithful to the wording of
Scripture there is no warrant, either in the Old Testament or
the New, for any such connection between Genesis vi and the
two New Testament texts just mentioned. We owe it to that
apocalyptic pseudepigraph, the Book of Enoch.

WHO THEN WERE THOSE "SONS OF GOD"?

But now, having shown the error and the origin of this "angel"
theory, it is time we gave a positive answer to the question:
Who were those sons of God in Genesis vi? We give our answer
unhesitatingly: *They were the men of the Seth line.* We maintain
that this is the true answer on three grounds: (1) the setting
and the wording of the passage, (2) the weakness of the objections, (3) the untenableness of any suggested alternative.

The Setting and the Wording.

It is most important to see the two occurrences of the expression, "the sons of God," in Genesis vi. 2 and 4, in their contextual connection. This is always the best safeguard against fanciful error. What then of the context? We submit the following considerations.

First; on reading through Genesis iv and v (the chapters which lead up directly to the "sons of God" crisis in chapter vi), we cannot fail to be impressed by the fact that *in the descent from Adam the Seth line is noticeably distinguished from the Cain line.* The writer of those chapters most evidently intends the reader to note this tracing down of Adam's descendants through the two distinct and separate lines. First we have the line through the outcast Cain, down to Lamech, the seventh man in the succession (iv. 16–24). Then we have the line through the elect Seth, down to Noah, the tenth man in the succession (iv. 25–v. 32). This distinction, even by itself, seems naturally to suggest that the distinction made immediately afterward, between the "sons of God" and the "daughters of men" is but the writer's continuing distinction between the two lines already mentioned.

Second; *the special features of the Seth line are such as to make the title, "sons of God," seem natural and appropriate to them.* Seth, as his very name means, was "appointed" to take the place of murdered Abel. Eve recognized this divine appointment in calling him Seth (iv. 25). This means that the Seth line was the *Messianic* line, the line from which the promised Redeemer should come (as indeed the Seth line actually proved to be, subsequently). The "Seed of the woman" who should "bruise the head" of the serpent was *not* to come of the Cain line, for that line was rejected. Cain was "of that wicked one" (1 John iii. 12). Seth and his sons, through the line of Enoch and Noah, were the chosen ones; that is, they were the line of God's *elect*, through whom the divine purpose ran. How understandable, then, that *these* should be called "the sons of God"!

Third; *the moral traits of the Seth line, in contradistinction to those of the Cain line, make the title, "sons of God" still more appropriate.* Take the Cain line first. Cain himself was a murderer.

He was also a man of the earth, earthy. All his aspirations were earthy. He "went out from the presence of the Lord" (iv. 16). Thenceforth there is not a mention of God or of worship in the Cain line. With the seventh man of this line, Lamech, we find polygamy, murder, and a godless boastfulness (iv. 19, 23, 24). How different is the Seth line! At the very beginning Seth himself is recognized as a special appointment of God (iv. 25). We are told also that Seth was begotten in Adam's "own likeness" (v. 3), which means that the contrast which existed between *Cain* and the original nature of Adam did not exist between *Seth* and Adam. Seth was more nearly in that beautiful, original image. Again, we are told that Seth had a son named Enos, and that "then (evidently led by Seth and Enos) began men to call upon the name of Jehovah" (iv. 26), a statement which has been badly bandied about by expositors, but which simply means that men then began most definitely to worship God, as we can easily see from Genesis xii. 8, xiii. 4, xxi. 33, xxvi. 25, where precisely the same words occur in the Hebrew as well as in our English translation. And still further, with the seventh man of this line, Enoch, we find (in utter contrast with the seventh man of the Cain line) the most beautiful example of godliness anywhere recorded: "Enoch walked with God; and he was not; for God took him." If all these considerations do not make it clear that the Seth line were the true worshippers of God, the spiritually-minded men, and that the designation, "sons of God," befitted them, then we are strangely mistaken!

Fourth; it is surely made clearer still that "the sons of God" in chapter vi were the men of the Seth line, *by the remarkable development of the narrative from chapter iii to chapter vii*. There is much that we could wish we knew about the antediluvian age; but the narrative is severely reticent. Sixteen hundred years are packed into two-and-a-half pages. It is as though the inspired author or compiler was anxious above all else that we should not miss seeing the connection between the Fall and the Flood. Thus, in chapter iii we have the Fall. Next, in chapter iv we are shown the Cain line. Next, in chapter v we are shown the Seth line. Next, in chapter vi *the two lines cross* (*i.e.*, "*the sons of God*" with "*the daughters of men*," etc.). Finally, in chapter vii there comes the judgment of the Flood. The development from the Fall to the Flood is presented in almost dramatic form. The movements are drawn with such vividness that to our own mind, at least, there seems no possible doubt as to the writer's intention. He means us to see the breakdown of the vital separation between the two lines; and if this is so, then "the sons of God" must be the men of the Seth line.

So much for the context; but besides this *the wording and the incidental references of Genesis vi confirm that these "sons of God" were the men of the Seth line.* Take verse 1, which says, "And it came to pass when men began to *multiply* on the face of the earth . . ." If the "sons of God" were the Sethites, then we can well understand why the ill-fated intermarriages took place only after men had thus begun to multiply, for the hitherto separated lines were now brought geographically near each other, and mutual intercourse was engendered. But if these "sons of God" were angels, why had *they* to wait all those hundreds of years before seeing "the daughters of men that they were fair"? The explanatory clause of that first verse just does not fit to angels.

Take verse 2. Surely the very expression, "sons of God" indicates that the persons concerned were *not* angels. Certainly this is so if Moses was the writer of the Pentateuch. We ourselves accept the conservative view that Moses was the author of the Pentateuch substantially as we have it. No less than fifteen times in the Pentateuch angels are referred to; and they are always called angels, never once "sons of God." If we accept the general Mosaic authorship of the Pentateuch, then it certainly seems as though the word "angels" would have been used in Genesis vi. 2, if angels had been meant.

But glance again at verse 2. It says that the "daughters of men" were "fair." Assuming that this refers to the daughters of the Cain line, it finds at once an incidental confirmation in chapter iv. 22, where we are told that Lamech's daughter was called *Naamah*, which means "beautiful."

And yet further, in verse 2, we read that "the sons of God saw the daughters of men that they were fair, and *they took them wives of all which they chose.*" Now surely this assumes that these "sons of God" were persons already on earth, as were the sons of Seth. There is not a single word or even the faintest hint that these "sons of God" somehow *came* to the earth for the purpose, much less is there the slightest suggestion that they were falling angels committing a staggering monstrosity. Surely had the latter been so, the writer would at the very least have said that they "came" or "descended" or "appeared," instead of simply "saw" and "took"!

Nor is that all in verse 2, for it says that the "sons of God" took them *wives.*" This is the usual word for the proper marriage relationship. Now, as the Imperial Bible Dictionary says, "Even carnal intercourse between such parties (angels and women) had been impracticable, but the actual taking of wives is still more abhorrent to the ideas set forth in Scripture as to the essential distinctions between the region of spirits and the world of sense." Surely, the idea that angels should not only have taken bodily shape, but should have done so permanently, and lived as husbands of human wives, and toiled for their living, and reared families, is preposterous the more one thinks of it! And to say that the *Nephilim* were the prodigy-offspring of such angel-human wedlock is simply wresting the Scripture, for verse 4 plainly says that the *Nephilim* were in the earth *before* the "sons of God" took wives of all which they chose.

And once again in verse 2, "they took them wives *of all which they chose.*" This is the marrying and giving in marriage to which our Lord Jesus refers (Matt. xxiv. 37, 38; Luke xvii. 26, 27). It is of this that Jesus says, "As it was in the days of Noah, so shall it be also" at the end of the present age. But if Genesis vi is the account of what *angels* did, there is no parallel at all between then and the predicted age-end days.

Glance now at verse 4. Our Authorized Version renders it, "There were giants (*Nephilim*) in the earth in those days." Now the word *Nephilim* does not in itself mean giants; and it is good that our later versions have not so given it. (The Authorized Version gives "giants" simply because it follows the Septuagint translation, already mentioned; and the Septuagint so rendered it because the *Nephilim* mentioned in Numbers xiii were evidently men of great stature.) Now those who hold to the *angel* theory regarding Genesis vi explain that the word *Nephilim* does not necessarily mean giants, but rather the *fallen ones*, from the

Hebrew verb *naphal*, which means "to fall." They then say that the *Nephilim* were thus the fallen ones, that is, the fallen angels, alias "the sons of God."

But alas for them, verse 4 doubly refutes that. First, it makes absolutely clear that the Nephilim were on earth *before* ever the "sons of God" fell to "going in unto the daughters of men" (so that if the *Nephilim* were the "sons of God" we are brought to the absurdity that they were the "fallen" ones *before they fell*!) Second, according to the best Hebrew scholars, *naphal* does not mean merely to *fall*, but to "fall *upon*," thus indicating violence (see Gesenius, Calvin, Kurtz, Keil, Edersheim and others). These *Nephilim* were men of violence, and any thought of size or stature is secondary, though it is probable, of course, that their violence was made the worse by reason of outstanding physical build. However, the simple point we here make is that once again, if we rule out the idea of angels, and see that these Nephilim were *violent men*, we have incidental corroboration in the narrative, and in this case it is verse 11—"the earth was filled with *violence*." If we say that they were *angels*, once again we have to start distorting the words of Scripture to make them fit a theory.

But then the whole chapter is against the "angel" theory. Verse 5 says: "And God saw that the wickedness of MAN was great in the earth." Verse 7 says: "I will destroy MAN . . . for it repenteth Me that I have made them." Verse 13 says: "The earth is filled with violence through THEM (men)." No mention or hint anywhere of angels! From all this are we not justified in saying that the wording and the setting of Genesis vi make abundantly clear that the "sons of God" were the godly sons of the Seth line?

THE WEAKNESS OF THE OBJECTIONS

What are the objections which can be brought against the view that the "sons of God" were the godly sons of Seth? Well, such as they are, no one has ever marshalled them with more force and fulness than the great German scholar, Kurtz. We have carefully read all that he says on the matter, and are much impressed by the weakness of it. Let us note the main objections.

First; he says it is decisive against us that "the sons of God" are placed in contrast with "the daughters of men" in general, and that therefore "the sons of God" must by contrast be *other than human*. Yet it is simply gratuitous to say that these contrastive expressions necessitate a contrast between the angelic and the human. Why, on practically the same basis Kurtz and Bullinger would be compelled to contradict their own "explanation" of verse 4 ("There were the *Nephilim* in the earth in those days; and also, after that, when the sons of God, etc."). Both Kurtz and Bullinger say that the *Nephilim* and the "sons of God" are identical. But why then does the inspired historian so awkwardly stick the two titles for the same persons on top of each other? Why does he not simply say: "There were the *Nephilim* in the earth in those days; and also, after that, when *they* came. . . ." The "they" would have been quite enough, without his clumsily inserting "sons of God," if the two expressions meant the same thing. To our own mind, the use of the two terms here indicates that the *Nephilim* and the "sons of God" are *not* identical; yet Kurtz and Bullinger find no difficulty in letting *these* contrastive titles refer to the same persons! Why, then, in view of the distinctive features and godly characteristics of the Seth line, should not verse 2 call them "sons of God" as a mark of special distinction from "the daughters of men" in general, without having to mean that they could not also be human?

An illustration may help. A tribal chief named Adma has two sons, whom we will call B and C. The former (B) is a rebel. The other (C) is loyal. The father therefore decrees that the tribal rights and title shall run in the line of C, which line becomes known as that of the "Loyalists"; and that line is to be kept separate from the other. Both lines are lines of Admas (from the name of the father), but one is distinctively the "Loyalists." As the two lines increase, the "Loyalists" see the daughters of the Admas that they are fair, and, instead of keeping to their own line, they take them wives of all which they choose. But does this mean that they themselves are no longer Admas? Not at all! And in exactly the same commonsense way may the sons of the Seth line be called distinctively the "sons of God"— the loyalist line both to Adam and to God—in Genesis vi. 2.

Kurtz's next objection is that the expression, "sons of God," is used only of angels, in the Old Testament. But, as we have already pointed out, the expression occurs *only four times* (Job i. 6, ii. 1, xxxviii. 7; Dan. iii. 25). Even of these, only the first two are identical with Genesis vi. 2, and even these two are held by some to refer to men, not angels (see Appendix). The expression, in the Daniel citation refers to One who was in *human* form, in the fiery furnace, as we have already pointed out. Moreover, in the Pentateuch, the uniform way of referring to angels is by the *word* "angels." If the title, "sons of God," in Genesis vi. 2 *does* mean angels, it is certainly a solitary exception.

But we may even turn this objection back upon the objectors, for in the New Testament the title "sons of God" (in the exact Greek equivalent of the Hebrew) is used again and again of *men*, that is, of the regenerate in Christ. Both Pember and Bullinger "explain" this as being because all who are the direct creation of God are called His "sons," and the new nature which is in us as regenerate believers is a direct creation of God. So the regenerate are "sons of God." Look back, then, over the Seth line. Were not the worshipping Seth and Enos and the sanctified Enoch and the "just" and "perfect" (upright) Noah who "walked with God"—were not *these* men regenerate? Who will dare to say "No"? And were they not, then, truly "sons of God"?

Third; it is argued by Kurtz that the necessity to destroy the whole race can only be accounted for on the angel-outrage theory. When God commenced a new race with *Abraham* He did not deem it needful to destroy all others: then why did He deem it needful when He started a new race with *Noah*? To our own mind, all such arguments, that if the circumstances were so-and-so, God ought to have done so-and-so, are unwise presumings; but at any rate, in this present instance, the objection obviously carries its own refutation. Why did God *spare* Sethite Noah at all? Verse 9 tells us: "Noah was a just man, and *perfect in his generations*"; that is, he (a *man*—nothing to do with angels!) had kept himself pure and separate from the mixed marriages and polygamy and sexual compromises of the time (which, once again, incidentally, carries the implication that it was for the sinning of *men*, not of angels, that the Flood came).

Kurtz's argument that the Flood was necessary because of an immoral incursion of angels is really absurd, for if *that* was the trouble, it would be the biggest of all arguments why a Flood to destroy *mankind* was *not* the right or necessary thing. Why did not God simply destroy the sinning *angels* and their unholy (supposed) brood, and, in justice, spare outraged mankind? (see also Appendix).

The only other objection of Kurtz worth mentioning is his attempted re-rendering of verse 4. We cannot but feel a tinge of shame that such a first-rank scholar should have tried to wring a forced meaning to fit a theory; but this is how he would alter the verse:

> "*There were Nephilim in the earth in those days and that just after the sons of God came in to the daughters of men and they bare children to them. These are the men of renown which were of old.*"

According to this, the Nephilim, instead of being on earth *before* the sons of God came to the daughters of men, were the resultant offspring. They came "*just after*"! Alas, however, Dr. Kurtz's "Devised Version" will not do. We have looked up the best Hebrew scholars, and his rendering is wrong. Indeed, as even the ordinary reader can see, Dr. Kurtz cannot find a place for the little words, "also" and "when" (which both come in the Hebrew). Read the verse again, with these two words emphasized, and no more is needed to refute Dr. Kurtz:

> "There were Nephilim in the earth in those days; and ALSO (or MOREOVER), after that, WHEN the sons of God came. . . ."

We have seen another objection, this time in Bishop Ellicott's commentary. This commentary rightly rejects the "angel" theory, but brings the following objection against identifying the "sons of God" with the men of the Seth line: "No modern commentary has shown how such marriages (i.e., between Sethite men and Cainite women) could produce 'mighty men' . . . 'men of renown'." The answer is really so obvious that we are surprised at the query. In the Hebrew, the expressions, "mighty men" and "men of renown" do not indicate anything of abnormality. The first comes again and again in the Old Testament, to mean the doughty warriors in Israel's armies. The other does not occur so often, but Numbers i. 16 sets the sense of it for us: "These (heads of the tribes) were the *renowned* of the congregation, princes of the tribes of their fathers, heads of thousands in Israel." The two expressions mean no more than outstanding *men*—outstanding as warriors or popular leaders. And as for "no modern commentator" having shown how such mighty men or popular leaders could come from intermarriage between the men of the Seth line and the women of the Cain line, why, it does not *need* any showing! It is too obvious. The men who grew up from these intermarriages would be the men who were popular with both sides, who had friends and relatives in both the lines, and who blended in themselves the strongly developed and outstanding qualities of both posterities! They would have the intelligence and lawlessness of the Cainites added to the peculiar superiorities handed down from religious ancestors. In every age the greatest corrupters of religion and society have been the demoralized descendants of religious ancestors.

There is only one other objection we need mention. It is far from the weightiest, but it is the most daring. Over against our own argument that the angels, as bodiless spirit-beings, are absolutely incapable of sexual processes, it has been counter-argued that "the possibility of progeny in consequence of the influence of a spirit-being (i.e., of angels) may be inferred from the fact that the virgin (the mother of our Lord) conceived by the influence of the Holy Spirit." But such an inference, besides being utterly repellent, is absolutely wrong. The human nature of the eternal Word was begotten in the virgin mother by a direct *creative* act of the Holy Spirit; whereas no such creative power could possibly be ascribed to angels or to any other created being. Moreover, this absurd idea that the angels could have *remained* spirit-beings and yet have begotten physical progeny on earth leaves altogether unexplained the marital *desire* implied in the words, "the sons of God *saw the daughters of men that they were fair*, and they took them wives of all which they chose."

Such, then, are the main objections, so far as we know, against accepting the natural, straightforward conclusion that the "sons of God" in Genesis vi were the godly sons of Seth: and we do not hesitate to call them, in the words of Jeremiah, "broken cisterns that can hold no water."

UNTENABLENESS OF SUGGESTED ALTERNATIVES

But we must add a further word. Our conviction that those "sons of God" were the godly sons of Seth is finally confirmed by the untenableness of the suggested alternatives. There are four. We will take them in order.

First; there is the theory that they were *angels*. This idea, as we have now seen, is untenable for the following reasons: (1) It involves an absolutely insuperable psycho-physiological contradiction. (2) Careful examination shows that both the setting and the wording of Genesis vi are against it. (3) The title, "sons of God," need not be restricted to angels, as is argued, and it is certainly inappropriate to *fallen* angels. (4) Any identifying of the *Nephilim* either with angels or the "sons of God" is an outrage on the clear wording of the passage. (5) The supposed New Testament confirmation of the theory is found, on careful inspection, to be *only* suppositionary, and not real.

Second; there is the theory which many Jewish interpreters have sponsored, that the "sons of God" were persons of quality, princes and nobles, and that the "daughters of men" whom they married were females of low birth. This argument is based upon an idiom of the Hebrew language, in which there is no superlative. When the Hebrews would speak of a very great city or a very great wind or most excellent cedars, they would call them a "city of God," a "wind of God," "cedars of God." The expressions, "sons of God," should therefore be understood as "sons of the mighty." Thus Genesis vi would teach that the antediluvian princes took wives from the attractive women of the inferior class. Yet surely such an argument carries its own refutation. It would mean that the climax of corruption for which the Flood came was simply marrying below one's rank! No such stigma is attached anywhere else in the Bible to such condescension in wedlock—in such cases as that of Boaz and Ruth it is extolled!

Third; we may quickly dismiss the even stranger theory, fathered by Bishop Ellicott, that the "sons of God" were the descendants of Cain. Even the soundest and sanest of expositors can have lapses, yet even so it is strange to find Bishop Ellicott's commentary advocating such an interpretation of Genesis vi. On the basis of chapter iv. 17–24 he holds that the descendants of Cain were superior to the descendants of Seth in a civil and social and martial sense, that *they* were really the "sons of the mighty" or "sons of God." The Sethite men could not have taken the daughters of the Cain line, because the Cainites were too strong for them; but the Cainite men *could* take the daughters of the Seth line, because the men of the Seth line were inferior and unable to prevent them. But this idea is self-defeating. The Bishop rightly points out that the expression, "the daughters of men" is literally "the daughters *of the adam*," and he claims that the word "adam" here means the Seth line. But alas for him, the very next verse reads: "And the Lord said, My Spirit shall not always strive with *the adam*"—so that we get the strange contradiction of the Spirit striving with the innocent Sethites for what the naughty Cainites were doing!

Fourth; that eminent scholar, Delitzsch, who leaned toward the "angel" theory but perceived the insuperability of the psycho-physiological difficulty in relation to sexless spirit-beings like the angels, tried to take a sort of half-way position. He says: "They were demons who accomplished what is here narrated, by means of men whom they made their instruments, who with demoniacal violence drew women within the radius of their enchantments, and made them subserve the purpose of their sensual lusts." Yet in reality that is no half-way position; for if they were men who so acted, even though under the urge of evil angels, they were still men; so the "angel" theory breaks down. But what exegesis is it which makes "sons of God" into demon-possessed sensualists?!

Such, then, are the four suggested alternatives to the conservative view. We turn from them more convinced than ever that the "sons of God" in Genesis vi were the godly sons of Seth. We see the two clearly demarcated lines—the Seth line and the Cain line. We see that the Seth line is the Messianic line, the line of the elect. We see that the moral traits of the

Seth line give added appropriateness to the title, "sons of God."
We see the development of the narrative from Genesis iii to vii
adding confirmation. We see incidental corroborations in verse
after verse of the chapter, and in the words of our Lord Jesus
Himself concerning "the days of Noah." What is more (for we
have not mentioned this important point before), again and again
in the Scriptures we find the godly called the sons of God, even
though not in the exact Hebrew wording of Genesis vi. 2. Take
the following instances, in which the word "sons" is the same
Hebrew word as in Genesis vi. 2:

> "Ye are the sons of Jehovah"—Deut. xiv. 1.
> "Thy sons" (i.e., of Elohim)—Psalm lxxiii. 15.
> "Sons of the Most High"—Psalm lxxxii. 6.
> "Bring My sons from far"—Isaiah xliii. 6.
> "Thou hast slain My sons"—Ezekiel xvi. 21.
> "Sons of the living God"—Hosea i. 10.

But specially note Psalm lxxxii. 6 and Hosea i. 10, where the
expression "sons of *Elyon*" and "sons of *Elkhâyee*" is practically
the equivalent of "sons of *Elohim*" in Genesis vi. 2. And most
of all note the expression "Thy sons" in Psalm lxxiii. 15; for
all through this psalm the name of God is *Elohim* (verses 1, 26,
28) or *El* (verses 11 and 17), so that with utter clearness, "Thy
sons" means *sons of Elohim*. Surely this is the final knock-out
of the Pember-Bullinger claim that only angels are "sons of
Elohim"! Nor is even that all. Our Lord Jesus, using the exact
Greek equivalent of the Hebrew, says in Matthew v. 9, "Blessed
are the peacemakers; for they shall be called *the sons of God*."
This is the knock-out of the further Pember-Bullinger claim that
the expression is only used in the New Testament of those who
are Christian believers of the Church age distinctively. And
finally (though by no means necessary to us), if, as many think,
the "sons of God" in Job i. 6 and ii. 1 were not angels but godly
men (see Appendix), then the already-completed demolition of
the Pember-Bullinger idea is made the more pronounced.

THE ABIDING LESSON

So, then, the "sons of God" in Genesis vi. 2 were the godly sons of the Seth line. Let us therefore dismiss the fanciful "angel" theory completely from our minds. And if it should be in some minds to ask: What then of "the angels that sinned" and who are mentioned in 2 Peter ii. 4 and Jude 6? we would reply that there are not a few hints and clues given to us in Scripture on that score, into which we cannot go here, but which we briefly review in an Appendix to this study.

Let us not fail to appreciate the great and serious lesson of Genesis vi. As soon as we have settled it in our minds that those "sons of God" were indeed the men of the Seth line, we see ourselves confronted with a warning lesson which recurs again and again in the Scriptures, namely, *the vital need for the separation of the people of God from the people of the world.* We see this again in the out-calling and separation of Abraham and his family, and later in the segregation of Israel in Egypt. We see it again in the baneful influence of the "mixed multitude" who came up with Israel from Egypt, and again in the lapse of Israel's sons with Moab's daughters. We see it in the strict regulations imposed upon Israel in connection with the occupation of Canaan, in the sorrows and servitudes which accompanied Israel's later compromises, and culminatingly in the banishing of the tribes into exile.

The same lesson is brought home to us again and again, in the history of the organised Christian church from sub-apostolic times right down to the present day. It seems to be one of the most difficult lessons to learn; yet it is written large in stark, black letters right through the Scriptures and right through the centuries for us to read; and the neglect of it always issues in religious confusion, moral breakdown, and divine judgment.

This lesson needs heeding to-day by the Lord's people more than ever before in the history of the Church. There is a complexity about life to-day, a multiplicity of subtle inducements to a false "broad-mindedness," a herding of vast populations into small areas, a loose attitude to the authority of the Bible, and a sort of religious-flavoured humanism floating about every-where, all of which things make compromise easier to-day, perhaps, than ever before. Then, of course, there still persists the old plea that we simply must make concessions on this or that point if our message is to be acceptable at all to the worldly crowd. But we never really lift men by going down to their own level—not, at least, where moral principles are concerned. The call to us to-day is to renew our separation. All around us we see blurred principles and lowered morals, and the organised church seems stricken with spiritual paralysis. These things are the outcome of compromise. The "sons of God" are to be a separated people. Sonship and separation are two ideals which go together again and again in Scripture. Surely Paul had this in mind when he wrote his stirring challenge, in 2 Corinthians vi. 17:

"Wherefore, come out from among them, and be ye *SEPARATE*, saith the Lord, and touch not the unclean thing; and I will receive you, and will be a Father unto you, and ye shall be My *SONS AND DAUGHTERS*, saith the Lord Almighty."

APPENDICES

APPENDICES

ON THE NECESSITY FOR THE FLOOD

PERHAPS we ought to add a further word concerning Kurtz's argument that the necessity for the Flood, and the total destruction of the Adam race thereby, can only be accounted for on the supposition that "the angels who sinned" had perpetrated the sex outrage which he and his fellow-theorists predicate of them. We have already pointed out that if it was for the sinning of angels that the Flood came, then it was the sinning **angels** who needed judgment and destruction, **not** outraged mankind.

But there is a further remark of Kurtz's which we did not rebut. He points out that when God commenced a new race with Abraham, He did not deem it necessary to destroy all others. Why then did God find it necessary to destroy all others when He started a new race with **Noah**, unless it was for some monstrosity such as that which the angels (supposedly) committed?

Nothing is more easily disposed of than such speculative and hypothetical reasoning. All we need to do is to keep to the plain facts as given by the Bible. There is no parallel at all between the times of Noah and Abraham in this matter. Kurtz apparently clean forgets that there were three simply tremendous factors in the antediluvian age which no longer operated in the days of Abraham. These were (1) the extraordinary longevity of human life, which gave to perverted human nature extraordinary knowledge and power and opportunity for the committing of wickedness; (2) the existence of but the one, universal language among all the peoples of the earth, which also greatly facilitated collective and concerted evil-doing; (3) organized human government had not then been instituted: every man did that which was right or desirable in his own eyes.

In Abraham's time the duration of human life had been cut down almost to what it is to-day; and the "confusion" of language had been introduced at Babel; and the restraint of human government had been imposed. So there is simply no parallel between Noah's time and Abraham's. Moreover God would have violated His own covenant and promise if He had destroyed the race again in Abraham's time, for he had given to mankind the promise of Genesis viii. 21, 22, "I will not again curse the ground any more for man's sake; for the imagination of man's heart is evil from his youth; **neither will I again smite any more every thing living, as I have done.** While the earth remaineth, seedtime and harvest, and cold and heat, and summer and winter, and day and night shall not cease." Thus Kurtz's words fall to the ground.

ON THE "SONS OF GOD" IN THE BOOK OF JOB

As we have said, there are those who hold that the "sons of God" who "came to present themselves before the Lord," in Job i. 6 and ii. 1, were not angels but godly men. For instance, Mr. George Rapkin, in his book on Genesis says:

"We have, in the Book of Job, the statement in i. 6 and ii. 1, 'The Sons of God came to present themselves before the Lord.' The expression here for 'sons of God' is the same as in the Hebrew of Genesis vi. 2, namely, **beni ha Elohim**. It has been concluded by scholars that Moses was the author of the Book of Job, and that he (Job) lived in the Patriarchal period, probably before the Flood. Here, again, is the expression, ' the presence of the Lord.' Now can it be assumed that the angels are not always in His presence? But these **beni ha Elohim** were not always there, and came at a certain season for this purpose.

"The story of Job opens by telling of a devout father, who, when he knew his children were feasting, offered sacrifice for them, lest they should have blasphemed God. Then came the day of appearing before God, and of Satan being granted the permission to harass the father.

"The 'sons of God' were the godly men of the time who came for worship in the presence of the Lord. They came before the Lord just as David later urged the congregation to do, when urging thanksgiving. Coming before the Lord and entering His presence is not so striking when we find the Bible speaking of men and congregations doing this. Nimrod is said to have been a 'mighty hunter before the Lord,' but we do not stretch our fanciful imagination to the extent of saying he must have been an angel. Now Job and his sons, with other righteous men, were the sons of God who presented themselves before the Lord for the act of worship and sacrifice, the father then acting as the head, or priest, of the family worship and sacrifice."

Mr. Rapkin is by no means alone in holding this view. It is surprising how much may be said for it. The Book of Job is perhaps the oldest in the Bible. It goes right back to earliest times, when there seems to have been visible manifestation of the divine presence among men, in connection with their worship. These "sons of God" in Job came before "the presence of Jehovah." and it was from the same "presence" that "Satan went forth." It is just the same expression as in Genesis iv. 16, where we read that "**Cain** went out from the presence of Jehovah"; and just the same as with **Jonah** who fled "from the presence of Jehovah" (Jonah i. 3, 10).

Now no one would say that Cain or Jonah were going out from some audience with God **in heaven**! They were both quite definitely on earth, and they passed out from some **visible presence of God on earth** (which, incidentally gives the lie to those who stupidly imagine that Jonah thought he could escape from the **general** presence of God. Jonah's own words in verse 9 should have shown them otherwise). So, it is consistently argued, the "sons of God" in Job were not angels coming before God in heaven, but godly men coming before Jehovah on earth. It is also pointed out that the coming into "the presence of Jehovah" was **voluntary** ("the sons of God came to **present** themselves before Jehovah"); so that this was no compulsory reporting of angels and Satan to God. It is pointed out still further that they came before **Jehovah**, which is especially a name of God toward **man.** And there are other arguments. We do not say, for the moment, whether we ourselves accept this view; but certainly, if it be true, then that most confident of all the Pember-Bullinger arguments, that the title "sons of God" refers only to angels, falls in complete ruin.

ON THE ANGELS THAT SINNED

If, as we have now shown, the "sons of God" in Genesis vi. were **not** the "angels that sinned" (2 Pet. ii. 4) and which "kept not their first estate" (Jude 6), then **when** did that fall of angels take place? This is a question which is certain to have arisen in some minds.

A preliminary caution is wise, perhaps, on such a subject: We must be careful not to mix human speculation with divine revelation. About such a matter we can only know just what the Spirit of inspiration has been pleased to reveal; and there is a marked reserve about it in Scripture.

The "Scofield" Bible comment on the words of Genesis i. 2, "And the earth was (became) without form and void," is worthy of note:

" Jeremiah iv. 23–26, Isaiah xxiv. 1 and xlv. 18, clearly indicate that the earth had undergone a cataclysmic change as the result of a divine judgment. The face of the earth bears everywhere the marks of such a catastrophe. There are not wanting intimations which connect it with a previous testing and fall of angels. See Ezekiel xxviii. 12–15 and Isaiah xiv. 9–14, which certainly go beyond the kings of Tyre and Babylon."

We know that Satan's own fall was before the beginning of human history. It seems quite clear, also, that he was a prince and leader among the angels, with great influence among them, even as he is now the commanding power over fallen angels who operate along with him. In Psalm lxxviii. 49 we read of "evil angels." In Matthew xxv. 41 we read of "the devil and his angels." In Revelation xii. 3, 4, we read of the "dragon" whose "tail drew the third part of the stars of heaven"; and the ensuing verses interpret the "dragon" and these "stars" as "the devil" and "his angels" (7, 9), who fight against "Michael and his angels," but "prevail not."

We read also of evil spirit-beings, or more probably **combines** of spirit-beings, named "principalities and powers in the heavenlies," and "world-rulers of this darkness, the spiritual hosts of wickedness in the heavenlies" (Eph. iii. 10, vi. 12, R.V.); and Satan is clearly revealed as the leader of all these, for he is called "the prince" (or ruler) of all this "power (or authority) of the air" (Eph. ii, 2).

He is also the leader of the " **demons** " ("Beelzebub, the prince of the demons," Matt. xii. 24–6), and these are so numerous as to make Satan's influence practically ubiquitous (see Mark v. 9, where the demon-spirits are called "Legion", an indication of their numerousness and their organized warfare). These "demons" may be the same as the evil angels, though that is a point on which there is not absolute certainty. But, it is abundantly clear that over all these various spirit-beings and combines Satan is lord and leader.

It is also clear that this awful being has **special relationship with this world.** Our Lord Jesus calls him "the prince (or ruler) of this world" (John xii. 31, xiv. 30, xvi. 11). In 2 Corinthians iv. 4 he is called "the god of this age." It was he who, at the very beginning, inveigled our first parents, in Eden, thus bringing about the sin and fall of mankind. Away back in the Book of Job, also, we see him "going to and fro **in the earth** " (Job i. 7, ii. 2).

All these considerations, especially when taken with certain Old Testament passages which we shall now mention, make it easy to believe that in pre-human eras Satan (as yet unfallen) may actually have been the rightful and divinely-appointed prince of this earth, presiding over an anterior species of beings; and it may even be that the very constitution of this earth was different then from now.

Referring again, then, to the Ezekiel passage which the "Scofield" note cites, we ourselves think it is quite clear that the phraseology takes us right beyond the king of Tyrus and indicates a latent reference to an angelic being of highest order, directly created by God. Read the words again:

"Thou sealest up the sum, full of wisdom and perfect in beauty.
"Thou hast been in Eden the garden of God; every precious stone was thy covering. . . .
"Thou art the anointed cherub that covereth; and I have set thee so; thou wast upon the holy mountain of God; thou hast walked up and down in the midst of the stones of fire.
"Thou wast perfect in thy ways from the day thou wast created, till iniquity was found in thee. . . .
"Thou hast sinned; therefore I will cast thee as profane out of the mountain of God; and I will destroy thee, O covering cherub, from the midst of the stones of fire.
"Thine heart was lifted up because of thy beauty; thou hast corrupted thy wisdom by reason of thy brightness: I will cast thee to the ground. . . .
"Thou hast defiled thy sanctuaries by the multitude of thine iniquities, by the iniquity of thy traffic; therefore will I bring forth a fire from the midst of thee, it shall devour thee, and I will bring thee to ashes upon the earth."

It is noteworthy that the expression in verse 18, "Thou hast defiled thy sanctuaries," is in the singular in many Hebrew manuscripts—"Thou hast defiled thy **sanctuary,**" and it immediately sets up a connection in our minds with Jude's words about the angels who "left their own **habitation.**"

Then, of course, there is that even more arresting passage, in Isaiah xiv. 9–15, which equally evidently has an underlying mystic reference to Satan, to his pre-adamite fall and his subsequent evil princedom over the present world-system.

> "Hell from beneath is moved for thee to meet thee at thy coming: it stirreth up the dead for thee, even all the chief ones of the earth: it has raised up from their thrones all the kings of the nations. . . .
> "Thy pomp is brought down to the grave, and the noise of thy viols: the worm is spread under thee and the worms cover thee.
> "How art thou fallen from Heaven, O Lucifer, son of the morning! how art thou cut down to the ground, thou that didst weaken the nations!
> "For thou hast said in thine heart, I will ascend into Heaven, I will exalt my throne above the stars of God.
> "I will ascend above the heights of the clouds; I will be like the Most High.
> "Yet thou shalt be brought down to hell, to the sides of the pit."

We know, of course, that there are scholars who would limit these passages in Ezekiel and Isaiah simply to Tyrus and Babylon. But there is a scholarship which is merely of the letter; and when we think of other passages like Psalm xxii and Isaiah liii (not to mention many others) where the same sort of latent mystic significance is interwoven with the more immediate reference to local and historical happenings of long ago, we cannot but sense that in Ezekiel xxviii and Isaiah xiv there is this deeper reference to Satan.

Besides, even when we have allowed for poetic licence or florid Orientalism, some of the expressions simply cannot be limited to Tyrus or Babylon. For instance, to pick just one such expression out: "I will exalt my throne above the stars of God." We have seen how the "stars of heaven" in Revelation xii are angels. So is it in Job xxxviii. 7, where we read that "the morning stars sang together." But whether the "stars" in Isaiah xiv are angels or literal stars, the king of Babylon never envisaged such a conquest as that! And still further, these latent references to Satan tally (too clearly for us not to notice) with the many other hints and clues and statements scattered through the Scriptures concerning Satan.

And what do we learn from these passages when taken with the various other revelations of Scripture concerning Satan and the fallen angels and other evil spirit-agencies? Well, first we see clearly that the fall of Satan was **before** the creation of man. Second, the fall of the evil spirit-powers over whom Satan is prince is connected with Satan's own fall, and presumably happened at or about the same juncture. Third, the wreckage of the earth which we find recorded in Genesis i. 2 was probably the result of a divine judgment on this rebellion of Satan and angels; especially does this seem so when read in conjunction with Jeremiah iv. 23–28, and Isaiah xiv. 18, which says that originally God did **not** create the earth in vain (literally "without form" as in Gen. i. 2). Fourth, there is absolutely **no word or hint or suggestion of any fall of angels subsequent to the beginning of human history.**

We need say no more along this line. Speculation is easy and tempting: but enough has been said to show that the fall of angels spoken of in 2 Peter ii. 4, and Jude 6 may well have taken place in that pre-adamite era, and may have coincided indeed with the fall of Satan himself.

DATE DUE

0.7
55s
60

RY
0